W9-CHP-903

Political Hermeneutics

The Early Thinking of Hans-Georg Gadamer

Political Hermeneutics

The Early Thinking
of
Hans-Georg Gadamer

Robert R. Sullivan

The Pennsylvania State University Press
University Park and London

Quotations from Hans-Georg Gadamer's *Dialogue and Dialectic*, trans. Christopher Smith, reprinted with permission of Yale University Press, © 1980 Yale University Press.

Quotations from Hans-Georg Gadamer's *Gessamelte Werke*, vol. 5, reprinted with permission of J. C. B. Mohr (Paul Siebeck), Tübingen, Copyright © 1985 J. C. B. Mohr (Paul Siebeck).

Library of Congress Cataloging-in-Publication Data

Sullivan, Robert R.
Political hermeneutics.

Includes index.
1. Gadamer, Hans Georg, 1900–   —Contributions in political science.
2. Gadamer, Hans Georg, 1900–   —Contributions in hermeneutics.
I. Title.
JC263.G35S86   1989   320.5   88–43435
ISBN 0-271-00670-6

To the Memory of My Father

Francis T. Sullivan
1911–1983

Contents

Preface

This book was written over several years and has incurred for
the author numerous debts. Hans-Georg Gadamer was always
generous with his time and kind in his treatment of initially
tentative interpretations. He is certainly one of the finest conversationalists of our time, and I am in his debt for that experience. I am also grateful to Thomas McCarthy of North-
western University and Hans Aarsleff of Princeton University
for getting me started and keeping me going on this project.
Two summer grants from the National Endowment for the
Humanities and equal number of City University of New York
Professional Staff Congress grants were also helpful and are
much appreciated. For incisive critical commentary, I am very
much in the debt of Richard Palmer of MacMurray College
and Fred Dallmayr of Notre Dame University.

For helpful criticism, friendly comments, or simply good
conversation related to the topics that structure this book, I
would also like to thank Professors Ed Davenport and Hilail
Gilden of the City University of New York and Professors

Horst-Jürgen Gerigk and Imre Toth of the Universities of Heidelberg and Regensburg, West Germany. I am also endebted to Elaine Bert, my department secretary, for cheerfully and efficiently doing numerous unseen tasks and to my institution, John Jay College of the City University of New York, and the CUNY Graduate Center, for providing support services.

Mostly, however, I am in the debt of my wife, Karin. Not so much because she kept the children quiet and did the typing, neither of which was especially the case, but because as an artist she understood philosophical hermeneutics in a way that no academic intellectual in my experience ever has. She did not have to conceptualize philosophical hermeneutics in order to live it. Rather, she lived it on a daily basis in her art, thereby providing a source for my conceptualization.

Needless to say, the interpretation that knits the following pages into a book is my own and should not be held against any of the above-mentioned persons. Similarly, factual errors, which hopefully are few, are traceable to the author alone.

I would like to acknowledge and thank Yale University Press for permission to quote from *Dialogue and Dialectic* and J. C. B. Mohr (Paul Siebeck) for permission to quote extensively from volume 5 of Gadamer's *Gesammelte Werke*.

1

Introduction
to the
Early Gadamer

I

Hans-Georg Gadamer is a contemporary German philosopher best known in Europe and the United States as the creator of philosophical hermeneutics, a direction of thought that raises a skeptical voice about knowledge claims in the modern world. This admittedly dry description of philosophical hermeneutics can easily be dramatized: If humans are historically situated beings, as Martin Heidegger taught, then it follows that certain knowledge of the human condition is neither possible nor desirable. As Gadamer puts it, our historical situatedness mandates that knowledge begin in something that became disreputable in the seventeenth-century scientific Enlightenment: our prejudices. To be sure, responsibility to our own selves and to each other also mandates that we not act on prejudices before we rigorously test and establish them as judgments. Yet even these outcomes, much as we prize them, are not valid for all eternity. They are not certain knowledge. With the passage of time—that is to say, with the unfolding of our historical situatedness—every judgment once again becomes a prejudgment, or prejudice, and so the aging process invariably obligates our species to return to its humble non-epistemological origins. This argument, presented here in thumbnail sketch, is a direct challenge to the modern European Enlightenment.

Gadamer's major book is *Truth and Method*, first published in the German original in 1960, when the author was sixty years of age.[1] It laid out the case for philosophical hermeneutics. Since then, and since the American edition in 1975, other writings have been published and translated. They function mainly to elaborate the argument made in *Truth and Method*. The work called *Philosophical Hermeneutics* is not a book in any consistent sense but is rather a collection of smaller, previously published pieces that comment on one or another aspect of the title's theme.[2] *Dialogue and Dialectic* is a collection of Gadamerian writings, all dealing with Plato and Platonic thinking.[3] Some of the pieces collected here are from Gadamer's early career, but they are not treated as being distinct from the direction he carved out in his 1960 book. They are rather treated as illustrations of Gadamer's art, and hence are already subject to a distorting interpretation.

Similarly, *Hegel's Dialectic* is a collection of small, for the most part recent writings on Hegel's thought, and *Reason in the Age of Science* is yet another collection of recent and not so recent writings.[4] In contrast, the work entitled *The Idea of the Good in Plato and Aristotle* is a long essay written by Gadamer late in life, and *Philosophical Apprenticeships* is a memoir-autobiography rather than a philosophical treatise.[5] The point, in brief, is that the Gadamer known to us in the United States has written only one real book, now translated into more than a dozen foreign languages, and the other books are compilations or marginal efforts dependent for their success on the reputation the author had already established for himself in his *magnum opus*.

Why then write a book on the early writings of Hans-Georg Gadamer? Will this not simply and inevitably be a commentary on the long gestation period of *Truth and Method*? Does Gadamer have anything to say in his early writings that is other than a premature formulation of his 1960 argument? The answer is suggested by the sketch already given of Gadamer's American reception history.[6] By publishing *Truth and Method* first and everything else thereafter, the makings of a distorted reception were created. And the distortion is not without significance for this volume: It creates one good reason for taking a hard look at Gadamer's early writings on their own terms. But first, let me establish what those early writings were.

Gadamer completed his doctoral dissertation, called *Das Wesen der Lust in den platonischen Dialogen* (The Essense of Desire in Plato's Dialogues), in 1922.[7] Five years later, in 1927, he published his first journal article,[8] an academic piece drawn from the research being done on his habilitation thesis. The habilitation is a German institution that might best be described as a second and more elaborate doctoral dissertation, needed to qualify for the German professoriat. Gadamer's habilitation thesis was called *Platos dialektische Ethik* (Plato's Dialectical Ethics), and it was completed in 1928 and published as a book in 1931.[9] It qualified Gadamer for the German professoriat, although he did not actually get the call until 1938. Meanwhile, in 1934, Gadamer published a long essay on Plato's problematic relation with the poets,[10] and in 1942 a somewhat shorter essay on Plato's concept of an educational state.[11] The latter piece, according to Gadamer, was written in conjunction with the 1934 piece, although publication was held off for several years.[12] In between and along the way, he also published a long list of short reviews and review articles, three or four of which dealt directly with Plato or writings on Plato by Gadamer's contemporaries.[13] One of these reviews, called *"Die neue Platoforschung"* ("Recent Plato Research"), is significant for this book.[14] Another unpublished work, called *"Praktisches Wissen"* ("Practical

Knowledge") is also important.[15] These are Gadamer's early writings.

The collapse of Germany in 1945 drove a wedge into Gadamer's academic life and served to set apart the period from 1922 to 1945 as an early period. The sustained thinking he did on Plato in this period was returned to later, but only after Gadamer had published *Truth and Method* in 1960. The period from the end of World War II to 1949 was one in which Gadamer worked as an academic administrator in Leipzig and then, in Frankfurt, as professor and editor for Vittorio Klostermann. In 1949, he was called to Heidelberg to replace the departing Karl Jaspers, and now once again he regained the leisure to think and write. It was during this period that he began the work that would lead to *Truth and Method*. This span of years, rather than what came before it, is the gestation period of Gadamer's major work.

Let me first lay to rest the most likely interpretation of Gadamer's early period. This is the very understandable common-sense notion that Gadamer was acting out the first stage of a German academic career. He was, in sum, amassing a collection of related but still unsystematic publications which were motivated by the desire to impress the academic establishment and induce one or another recruitment committee to put out the "call," as Germans say. This argument is undeniably correct: The young Gadamer was as intent as any of his contemporaries in securing a tenured professoriat. Indeed, I get the impression that he was more intent than most. He wrote the book reviews that every young German academic wrote, traveled to conferences to see and be seen, cultivated relationships with the notables, took substitute positions, and scraped along on starvation wages. At the point where normal humans would have given up, Gadamer persisted.

But conceding this rather prosaic claim about career ambitions does not exclude the possibility that there might in addition be something more to Gadamer's early writings. In my opinion, there is a compelling internal logic to the writings Gadamer did in the twenty-year period from the early 1920s to the early 1940s. It is an elusive and incomplete logic, and as such it provides the materials for an interpretation that would complete it.

II

Though I will argue that the early Gadamer was well on the way toward establishing a model of discourse rationality that would stand over against the model of founded rationality familiar to the natural sciences and *Geisteswissenschaften* (human sciences) of Gadamer's youth, this does not seem to me to be the most compelling thread of Gadamer's early writings. Rather, those writings gain in internal coherence when one grasps them in terms of the classical model of political thinking, familiar to modern readers in Aristotle's analytical breakdown of ethics and politics as interrelated microcosm and macrocosm, also familiar in Plato's more nuanced and poetic references to large and, by implication, small signboards on the road to an understanding of justice. Now if this claim is to be redeemed, it has to be understood correctly. So let me sketch it out.

The logic of the argument runs as follows: In the German academic world at the end of the 1920s, it was fashionable to accept the authenticity of Plato's letters and argue that Plato had taken up philosophy as an alternative way of engaging in politics. Gadamer subscribed to this way of looking at Plato, for it allowed him to deny the doctrine of objective ideas and root Plato's thinking in something more worldly, more situated, and hence more accommodating to the notion of discourse rationality that the early Gadamer was wont to develop. This move enabled Gadamer to cultivate the literary figure of the "Platonic Socrates" and use this figure to defend the charge of intellectualism in Plato's moral philosophy. Gadamer simultaneously adopted the Aristotelian format of doing political philosophy and constructed his interpretation of Plato on its basis. For Aristotle, politics is a continuation of ethics, meaning in sum that desirable modes of acting at the individual level serve as reference points for the construction of the *polis*. The *polis* is the ethical individual writ large, in other words. In its turn, the *polis* then serves as reference point for the construction of the individual soul. Character is scribed, as it were, according to the ethical norms that body forth in the *polis*.

With this format in mind, Gadamer then wrote a book on Plato's ethics and followed it up with one unpublished paper and two major articles on Plato's treatment of the *polis*. Now although "Plato's Educational State" is obviously a treatment of politics, "Plato and the Poets" is not so clearly so. But it can be interpreted as such. It plays a pivotal role on the way to the vision of the educational state insofar as it clears the way or, differently stated, cleans up the transition between Plato's dialectical ethics and Plato's educational state. The early Gadamer was adopting an anti-establishment position on Plato's thinking and then reconstructing it in terms of the comfortable categories of Aristotelian ethics and politics. In this manner, Gadamer was a budding political thinker.

Was all of this done by the early Gadamer with tongue in cheek, in the Aesopian manner of someone who wanted to write about the collapse of established ethics in Weimar Germany and the rise of raw, unadorned power in Nazi Germany? The idea is an attractive one, and if for no other reason than to refute the suggestions that Gadamer might in some way have been accomplice to what was happening—through a relativistic philosophy, through an opportunistic careerism—I would like to be able to demonstrate that this was indeed the case. But my argument would be no more than speculation on the motivations of a young German academic.[16] I do not know what personally motivated Gadamer to concentrate for fifteen years on ethics and politics. I only know what is knowable, and that is the internal logic of a sequence of writings on Plato. If these shed light on the motivations of their author, they suggest that he was anything but a political authoritarian in his personal thinking.

Well and good, but for philosophical purists an interpretation of the young Gadamer as budding political theorist may come as a more perverse distortion than that provided by a more conventional version of his reception history. It calls primary attention to a format that must at best be judged secondary. If the later Gadamer had become a conscious political theorist, then the line of political interpretation sketched above, even if far-fetched in the initial impression it makes, would be of real interest. Gadamer, however, did not become a political theorist but rather became the originator of a school of philosophy called *philosophical hermeneutics.* Whatever else philosophical hermeneutics is taken as, it is not political theory, and it has had limited impact on contemporary political theorists. Its main impact has been in philosophy itself, where it has given heart to the so-called continental school of philosophy against the analytical tradition, and in literary theory and the philosophy of science. It has had and continues to have growing influence in the art world. It has had some impact on the philosophy of law, but it has still to the best of my knowledge not significantly influenced contemporary political philosophy.[17] Hence there is reason for going back over the same ground, viewing the political thinking as incidental and at best implicit rather than primary. In this view, the correct approach is to look for the budding hermeneutic philosopher in the early writings.

This of course can be done, and with some profit, but the outcome of the exercise is to reduce the early writings to a preview of coming attractions. Moreover, the danger is that the early writings will be viewed from the perspective of the chief concepts of *Truth and Method.* If, for example, the term "aesthetic consciousness" appears in an early writing, this will be interpreted as significant solely because it is the first instance of the use of a now-famous term. If, furthermore, the use of the term "aesthetic consciousness" was slightly different in 1934 from what it became in 1960, then so much the worse for the

1934 usage. It will be said that Gadamer developed from a clumsy early beginning to the mature stage of thinking he reached in 1960. The problem is of course immediately apparent. The past (Gadamer's past) is being interpreted in terms of the present. The interpretation is highly prejudiced, and one may have to go through complicated mental gymnastics to sustain it.

Hence, the exegetical approach itself presents significant problems. But it does have a singular advantage: The more I tried it out, the more I was persuaded to revert to the model of seeing the early Gadamer as a political theorist. When I did this, I produced a simpler and, for me, far more elegant interpretation. For example, the term "aesthetic consciousness," as it is used in the 1934 piece called "Plato and the Poets," functions to describe the effect of beautiful poetic language on the thinking of the Athenian people. It distracts them from the really significant problems and aspects of community and thereby paves the way for the disintegration of communal norms. They thus lose their political edge. Functioning in this way, the concept of "aesthetic consciousness" provides a mainstay of Gadamer's defense of Plato's exiling of the poets. Plato is intent on reforming the *polis*, and this is a matter of returning language to a more prosaic form so that it might better come to grips with the Athenian everyday. Politics in this sense is a matter of reforming language and consciousness to make them adequate to deal with the everyday problems of real life. Such a conception of politics really is a continuation of the dialectical ethics Gadamer sketched out in his habilitation thesis.

In other words, the discrepancy between the use of identical terms in the early and the later Gadamer could be more effectively explained by the notion that Gadamer was a political thinker (but perhaps not a "theorist") than by the notion that he was merely the still underdeveloped creator of philosophical hermeneutics. I had similar experiences with other concepts—for example, the term "play" as it is used in the habilitation thesis and elsewhere. In *Truth and Method*, the term "play" is very nearly developed into a concept that is usable as a tool wherever one chooses to employ it—in aesthetics, philosophy, law, or the like. In the early writings, it is always used more narrowly, which is to say that it is more situated and hence less of a concept. It describes a nonterminological quality of language which is desirable insofar as it is rooted in the need of the soul to sound itself out in its continuous effort to achieve *Gestalt*, or form. The notion of "play" in the early writings is virtually synonomous with the notion of "dialectical ethics" or an "educational state." It cannot easily be disengaged from its situatedness. So once again to the point: Gadamer's personal history, his life, as it were, was not simply a long preparation for the book he published in 1960. There was something different in the early Gadamer, and even if he had not continued it, I did not want to lose it.

My political interpretation of the early Gadamer in this book is also spelled out in terms of an academic conflict. It offers an interesting parallel to my political interpretation and is worth summarizing here. Classical philology (*Altphilologie*) in the Germany of Gadamer's youth was in a crisis. Over against an entrenched tradition of defining the field as a positivistic science there was a growing movement to return the field to its origins as an interpretive humanistic effort. *Altertumswissenschaft*, or the science of the ancient world, saw itself as a technical science equipped with powerful methods for establishing facts, which in turn would reveal patterns that would make sense of supposedly individual moments of genius. *Altertumswissenschaft* produced great works of scholarship, but it was increasingly ridiculed for forgetting just why it was that anyone would want to know Greece. The point was not to explain Plato but rather to present him in such a way that the full force of his thinking could live again. Schiller, the Schlegel brothers, and above all Hölderlin had understood this point one hundred and fifty years earlier, as had Nietzsche fifty years after Hölderlin. The point was to make Plato a model, or *Gestalt*, for young Germans. This direction laid the emphasis on interpretation at the cost of explanation, and the conflict provided a model that could be carried over to political thinking.

The term *politics*, in its modern usage, invariably suggests the presence of the state, and the state, as we know it, is a distinctly modern phenomenon. It is a centralized amassing of power that extends its determining and rationalizing influence into every aspect of everyday life. Its power is based on the industrializing economy and is closely allied with the scientific establishment. Its premise is that if the conditions of life can be controlled, then human action can be made predictable and hence governable. Modern political theory is distinguished as *modern* by its concern with the state. Either it wants to increase the power of the state or restrain an already amassed power by the development of a set of restrictions on the use of that power. In these respects, the early Gadamer is clearly not a *modern* political theorist.

Classical political thinking, in contrast to modern, is concerned with the *polis* rather than the state. It is, consequently, not really concerned with power and its methods of managing a human nature standing over against the state. Surely there are exceptional moments, such as in Thucydides' Melian dialogue, where interest is focused on power, or the opening speech of Thrasymachus in Plato's *Republic*, but these are exceptional moments, and in any case there is no question of management. The *polis* of classical political philosophizing rather stands "over against"—if that is the appropriate term here—the soul, and truth rather than method is the means by which it gives character to, rather than manages, the soul. For these reasons, the rationality of classical politics is finally based on language and conversation and not on any putative logic of human nature.

Reflection on the writings of the early Gadamer finally yields up an interpretation that does not fit any established category. The early Gadamer is a political thinker who is concerned with sketching in the outlines of the classical *polis* in terms not always palatable to the modern person. He starts at the microcosmic level of ethics, portrays a situation in which traditional values have failed, and attempts to construct a model of discourse rationality along the lines of which new ethical conclusions can be reached. Then he projects this model onto the macrocosm of the state. It gives him a critical framework for his 1934 piece on Plato and the poets and a prescriptive framework for his 1942 piece on Plato's educational state. Throughout there is a strong concentration of language, which goes hand in hand with a discourse model of rationality. It is in this sense that the early Gadamer is to be understood as a political thinker.

One last question brings me full circle to where I began: If the early Gadamer is so different from the later Gadamer of *Truth and Method*, then why did he change so greatly? My response may seem disingenuous but is not. I do not think the later Gadamer is all that different from the early. There is no "break" in the thinking of the two men. The basic structure of the early thinking is retained and presented anew in abstract form in *Truth and Method*. A good deal of enrichment is added, but this should come as no surprise. Implicitly, *Truth and Method* argues against founded rationality along much the same lines that the early Gadamer implicitly argued against the modern power state in his writings on Plato. Explicitly, *Truth and Method* argues a case, Gadamer's case, for the alternative of discourse rationality, just as the early writings argue the case for a dialectical ethics or a *polis* that rests finally on a "philosophical conversation." Nearly everything Gadamer wrote in his early period may be construed as an argument against founded rationality, above all against the concept of a rationality based on a nature that stands over against mind as "reality." In sum, against *method*, as that term emerged in the scientific revolution of the seventeenth century. His argument, construed positively, makes the case for discourse rationality, by which I mean a mode of thinking that seeks and finds whatever anchorage it has in the agreement of others in conversation. In sum, discourse rationality is

a matter of speech and finally language; it is a matter of philosophical hermeneutics. I do not think there is a decisive break
in the basic structure of Gadamer's thinking.

But my claim and argument in this book is not about the
later Gadamer. It is rather about the early Gadamer, and it is
time to see how that argument will unfold in this volume.

III

I am confident that in the Weimar period forms of discourse
rationality arose in all of the disciplines associated with the
human sciences, but it is inappropriate in a book limited in
scope by its focus on the writings of a philologian and philosopher to track them all. What is called for, it seems to me, is a
close look at the discipline from which the early Gadamer, the
engaged philosopher, took his inspiration. This field is philology, specifically classical philology (*Altphilologie*). Chapter 2
will provide an extended look at the development of established academic cultures and subcultures within the discipline
of classical philology in Germany. This chapter grew out of a
paper I gave at a National Endowment of the Humanities
Seminar at Princeton University. It provided me with the opportunity to deepen my background knowledge of the human
sciences in nineteenth-century Germany. It sets the stage for
the writings of the early Gadamer by showing to what extent
the study of classical philology was dominated by notions of
founded rationality, especially prevalent in the reception of
Plato.

Chapter 3 looks intensely at Gadamer's first publication
for the reason that it involved him in a friendly conflict with
Werner Jaeger, the then-reigning king of the classical philology establishment. Jaeger was an excellent philologist but left
something to be desired as a philosopher. This showed up in
his still well-known intellectual biography called *Aristotle*.[18]

At the core of Gadamer's quarrel with Jaeger is the attempt to show that a specific text of Aristotle was more a part of the oral tradition of discourse than the written tradition of academic writing. My point is that this little quarrel shows Gadamer trying to unfreeze a specific tradition of founded (written) rationality in favor of a tradition of discourse (oral) rationality. This introductory writing leads into Gadamer's habilitation thesis, which he was doing at the same time.

Chapter 4 is a recounting and a reflection of the theoretical sections of Gadamer's habilitation thesis. This work, which was published as Gadamer's first book in 1931, was a study of a late Platonic text and was carried out in a conventional academic manner. That is to say, Gadamer first set the stage in a long theoretical section or chapter, then he applied the standards he had established and defended to an actual case study. Now the text Gadamer chose, the *Philebus*, was of renewed interest in the academic world because it posed anew (thanks to Jaeger) the problem of Aristotle's relation to the later Plato. Gadamer wished to show, once again, that the later Plato was not becoming ossified into a founded rationalist. He was, at least when confronting ethical problems, openly engaged in a dialogue with himself, with the problem, and with others. In my terminology, he was something of a discourse rationalist.

I do not pay a great deal of attention to the actual analysis of the *Philebus*. I am more interested in the way Gadamer sets the stage for his treatment of this Platonic text, and what I hope to show is that Gadamer at this early stage of his career produced his first detailed philosophical hermeneutics. That is to say, he produced his first extended reflection on language and attempted to make the case for language as the means for thinking what we are doing. Key to this is the attempt to show that Plato is not a founded rationalist, proposing always the theory of ideas, but is rather a kind of discourse rationalist, falling back as it were on conversation and its agreements as the beginning and end of public rationality.

Let me pause to illustrate just what Gadamer is claiming that makes me characterize him as a discourse rationalist. His point, Gadamer tells us in a poetical moment in *Platos dialektische Ethik*, is not to show that Plato's ethics are dialectical but rather that dialectics are themselves ethical. I quote: *It will not be claimed here that Platonic ethics are dialectical but it will rather be asked in what sense the Platonic dialectic is ethics.*[19] This is a cautious, introductory (it is the fourth sentence of the original Preface) way of saying that Plato did not have a founded doctrine of ethical ideas which he then expressed in dialogue form. He rather invested all his energies into the development of a systematic dialogue form, which for Gadamer was itself ethical. In other words, Plato has no doctrine of founded ethical values which are to be expressed in the language of dialogue. This would turn language into a tool. Rather, dialogue itself is the ethical way of life because it is the manner in which we reflect on what we are doing and try to produce some normative, ethical conclusions about it.

Chapter 5 supports the conclusions tentatively reached in the previous chapter. It considers Gadamer's unpublished 1930 paper called *"Praktisches Wissen,"* which might best be translated as "Practical Knowledge." It draws a sharp distinction between Plato and Aristotle, making the latter the founder of *Begriffs* or analytical philosophy and Plato the practitioner of a "dialogical dialectics" which did not aim at the creation of an instrumental consciousness.

In Chapter 6 I am finally in a position to redeem my claim about the political content of Gadamer's treatment of Plato because I am finally in a position to consider "Plato and the Poets" (1934) and "Plato's Educational State" (1942). Here it is clear that Gadamer is adhering to the classical mode of political theorizing insofar as he is following his thinking about ethics with thinking about politics. These writings are too brief to be well developed. This I regret, if for no other reason than that it seems to weaken my case. But the weakening is purely material. It is the consequence of brevity rather than any change in Gadamer's argumentative course. In fact, each of these articles says as much as most books do about what is really important to the classical *polis*. I once asked Gadamer why he had not combined these two articles into a book and his response was that he had had precisely that intention in the early 1930s. But his stay in Marburg was interrupted by his substituting for Richard Kroner in Kiel, and after his coming back to Marburg he did not return to the study—more thought than research—on Plato's vision of an educational state. Only later did he put the unfinished work into the form of a paper and publish it.[20]

Chapter 7 is a conclusion in the normal sense of being a summing up and an attempt to redeem claims or at least draw conclusions from claims that were redeemed along the way. My point in this final chapter is that the early writings of Gadamer are well worth looking at if one bears in mind that Gadamer, like Max Weber in his essay "Politics as a Vocation," was responding to a real crisis. But where Weber was directly responding to the crisis of German politics in the twentieth century, Gadamer's response was indirect and so therefore my thoughts on it are mainly speculative.

Briefly, and on the basis of what has already been demonstrated, I attempt in this concluding chapter to distinguish Gadamer's thinking from Heidegger's and show why, on the basis of this thinking, Gadamer was anything but a Nazi. I also attempt an excursus in this final chapter by comparing Gadamer's thinking to that of Mikhail Bakhtin, viewing both thinkers from the perspective of the continental tradition of rooting thinking in something more humanistic than the analysis of human nature.

I believe this book will best show its worth if the following thought is borne in mind: the philosophical hermeneutics of the later Gadamer of *Truth and Method* is itself a relatively abstract concept. It is available to be applied to numerous fields, such as art, law, literary criticism, and the like. It possesses a universality and makes a universality claim that emphatically identifies it as a kind of *logos kath' auto* or autonomous philosophical concept. This is not the case with the political hermeneutics of the early Gadamer. The early writings present a more full-bodied version of philosophical hermeneutics, but in being full-bodied, the presentation is more earth-bound. As such, the political hermeneutics are not yet ready to be applied universally but remain rather a more finite three-dimensional, quasi-literary reflection on one experience, that of the soul in its partnership with the political community. Thus the early writings of Gadamer, his political hermeneutics, remind us that the study of politics before the advent of political science in the seventeenth century was a distinctly humanistic concern of transmitting and renewing Western values.

2

On the Philological Background
of
Gadamer's Early Writings

I

Hans-Georg Gadamer did his doctoral dissertation relatively
early in life, completing it in 1922 at the age of twenty-two.[1]
His doctoral adviser, Paul Natorp, was nearing retirement
at the time Gadamer worked with him, but the association
with Natorp was nonetheless significant for the shaping of
Gadamer's mind. Natorp was a first-rate thinker who had con-
centrated his efforts on modern science and on Plato scholarship. The latter effort had resulted in a controversial book
in 1902, called *Platos Ideenlehre*, in which Natorp had argued the unusual thesis that Plato had no doctrine of ideas in
the conventional sense of that term.[2] That is to say, Natorp
claimed that Plato did not believe in a realm of preexisting
objective ideas after which reality was formed. Rather, Plato
believed that ideas were more or less like hypotheses, or mental configurations—much like Kantian noumena—and this

meant that they were subjective conjectures to be tested for fit against a perceived reality.

The importance of Natorp's argument can be grasped by comparing it to Saussure's basically similar argument on the nature of language.[3] By arguing that language was irreducibly *arbitrary*, Saussure set the stage for the coming of linguistic relativity in modern language philosophy. What he meant was that a word did not have a preestablished meaning that endured through time. The meaning of a word depended fully on the context in which it was used. Therefore, meaning was context-bound, language was absolutely historical, interpretation was inescapable, and there was no method that could guarantee access to meaning prior to the actual use of a word. Similarly with Natorp, if Platonic ideas do not have objective meanings, then philosophy cannot be a matter of finding out what ideas mean and then using them accurately. The meaning of ideas is context-bound, ideas are therefore absolutely historical, and interpretation rather than method is the appropriate way to *do* philosophy. If ideas have no fixed meaning prior to their actual usage, then meaning is *arbitrary*—that is to say, it is attained in context—and hence philosophy can have no prior knowledge and must be interpretive, or hermeneutic.

The significance of this argument for Platonic philosophy is immense. It actually rearranges everything, for if there is no doctrine of objective ideas, then Plato is conceivably a political philosopher. That is to say, if ideas have no preestablished meanings, then the focus of Platonic philosophy necessarily shifts from knowledge of the meaning of ideas, which can be the preserve of a class of experts, to argument aimed at establishing meaning, or to a situation in which expertise necessarily means nothing more than a better capacity to marshal information and argue it more persuasively. From this point of view, a Platonic text is not telling us what an idea means. It is rather arguing what Socrates or Crito or Gorgias claims it means, and it is up to us—as readers—to go along with the argument and accept, reject, or modify what Plato intends.

Plato is a political philosopher because his texts locate themselves in this uncertain, changing, arbitrary world, and if he sometimes slips and seems to argue that an idea has "objective" or preestablished meaning, then this is only one more argumentative strategy that has to be taken from what it is worth. Politics, in this sense, is the ongoing attempt to determine meaning through conversation, and we do well to grasp in advance that every determination is a judgment which, with the passage of time, will be revealed to be arbitrary and hence a prejudice.

Natorp's book did not have a positive reception history. It argued against conventional German academic wisdom and hence posed a challenge to the German professorial establishment. Not surprisingly, numerous German academics took the book as an opportunity to establish their own orthodoxy by arguing in print against it.[4] By the same token, dissident academics in the field of Plato scholarship were attracted to Natorp because he provided the rare combination of an established name and deviant scholarship. This became even more the case when, toward the end of his life, Natorp began to be attracted to the writings of Rabindranath Tagore and Indian mysticism.[5] This influenced him to shift even more in his Plato thinking, emphasizing the humanism in Plato at the expense of the scientism. He first announced this shift to humanism in a talk given at the University of Berlin in 1913, but these ideas were not published until Natorp included them in revised form as part of a *"Metakritischer Anhang"* (Metacritical Supplement) to a second, postwar edition of his *Platos Ideenlehre.*[6]

Let me try to sum up Natorp's significance for the early writings of Gadamer: In the first two decades of the twentieth century, Natorp represented a resurgence of the forces which had originally inspired the rise of classical philology in Prussia over a century earlier. Along with Wolf, Hölderlin, Schiller, Humboldt, Schleiermacher, and above all Nietzsche, Paul Natorp represented the belief that the purpose of classical philology was *Bildung*, the education of the spirit through *Kul-*

tur, and that the best way to achieve this purpose was not through the positivistic accumulation of facts about the ancient world but rather through a reinterpretation of the great minds of Greece that placed emphasis on their creativity, and this meant placing emphasis on their language. Natorp thus drew Gadamer to one of two dominant trends of nineteenth-century German philology. In this chapter, I shall call that trend the *Bildungs* tradition, and I shall perhaps somewhat too persistently set it over against the positivistic tendencies of the opposed trend toward *Altertumswissenschaft*, an ungainly term perhaps best translated as Antiquity Studies. Both traditions have real problems, especially as they relate to political theory and practice, and so it might help to sketch them in detail as a deeper background to Gadamer's early thinking.

II

To get to the root of the *Bildungs* tradition it is best to go back one hundred and fifty years and locate its beginning in the thinking of Johann Gottfried Herder in respect to the study of language in Germany. Herder is doomed to be misunderstood as long as it is held that the purpose of language is to express *knowledge*.[7] Herder shifted away from this Enlightenment position and held that the purpose of language was to form the *self*, and for this end it was perfectly adequate.[8] If language were to record the emergence of self and the consciousness of self (*Selbst-bewusstsein*), then it had to be whole and filled with feeling, gestures, and action. If, on the other hand, language was understood to be a tool for passively expressing something that existed prior to it or outside it, whether this be Platonic "objective" ideas or knowledge or a pronouncement of the King of Prussia, then it was hardly adequate, especially in its poetic form. For the sake of knowledge, language had to become flat, sequential, prosaic, and analytical. Herder was in favor of the emergence or construction—the German word for which is *Bildung*—of the self through language, and for this purpose a holistic language of action was necessary.

Herder was not particularly interested in classical Greece, and so the application of his more general thinking to the specific contours of the Greek language was left to classical philologists, poets, and other hellenophiles. Wolf, Humboldt, Schiller, Hölderlin, Goethe, the Schlegel brothers and Schleiermacher in one fashion or another all adopted Herder's grasp of language and applied it to the Hellenes.[9] In respect to Plato, the application of Herderian thinking meant that the Platonic dialogues were no longer taken to be clumsy modes of expressing the Platonic doctrine of ideas. That is to say, the Platonic dialogues were not intent upon conveying knowledge; they are rather about the formation of the self. They were taken to be scenes in which the speaker was actively and expressively forming himself in words, and hence Plato was taken by this first generation to be a literary figure rather than a philosopher in the Enlightenment sense of the term.

Given what was earlier said about the political significance of reinterpreting Plato in this way, it is worth pausing to consider the *political thinking* of the creators of the German tradition toward which Gadamer would tend, although not adhere. Herder, Humboldt, Fichte, and of course Hegel all wrote about politics in a theoretical manner, but finally it was Schiller's writing that captured the idealistic spirit of the founding generation of the *Bildungs* tradition.[10] On the one hand, Schiller more than anyone else rejected the possibility of meaningful participation in the practical politics of the day in Prussia. It was not that reform could not be achieved. It was rather that reform was not enough. Schiller wanted a whole new foundation for politics, and this could be achieved only through *Bildung*, the most radical reconstruction of the German spirit. Schiller thus differed markedly from Humboldt, who certainly believed that reform of Prussia could be achieved, and if we are to locate the difference precisely, then we have to focus on the changing meaning of the term *politics*.

Schiller's envisioned polity contained within itself an interior contradiction. It was shaped in terms of the goal of the utmost cultivation of spirit (*Geist*), but spirit was so conceived that it could only develop by complete immersion in the classics of learning, and this meant complete withdrawal from the tawdry realities of everyday Prussian politics. The educational experience was to be sublime, and it was to result in the realization of a utopia here on earth, presumably somewhere in Germany. The main practical result of such a perfectionist scheme was to set the stage for what Fritz Stern has in one place called "the political consequences of the unpolitical German" and in another "the politics of cultural despair."[11] In other words, the political theory of the German *Bildungs* tradition exacted a high price to be calculated in terms of the political effectiveness of the educated middle classes, the *Bildungsbürgertum*. The Greeks, as they were imagined in the classical period at the end of the eighteenth century, symbolized an almost purely idealistic rationality, and the real meaning of this was that they were not political. The consequence of this attitude, when it was adopted by the *Bildungsbürgertum*, was to concede everyday politics fully, thus opening the way for the expansion of *Realpolitik*.

Moreover, the political theory of the *Bildungs* tradition was filled with potential for sharpening class differences, which were sharp enough anyway in nineteenth-century Germany. The definition of classical education was so extremely cultural as to exclude virtually everyone from the working classes, and the emphasis on actually learning the Greek language made it easy to test class background at any time one wished. Finally, the rejection of prosaic politics by the *Bildungsbürgertum* conceded to bureaucrats untouched by *Kultur* the actual day-by-day running of the German government and hence paved the way for a predictably uncultivated and mechanical rationalization of German society. In sum, the political consequences of the political theory associated with the *Bildungs* tradition were, to say the least, pregnant with the possibility for disaster.

There are few less plausible places to locate the origin of Gadamer's concept of *aesthetic consciousness* than in Schiller's essay on the "Aesthetic Education of Mankind," but curiously there is a dimension to Schiller's writing that would be retained by Gadamer. This was the notion, more an attitude than a clear idea, that *Kultur* would produce a being who would be truly creative, and such a person would be political in the most radical sense of the term. The same notion is at work in the most distant of Humboldt's writings, such as his piece on the Cavi language, where Humboldt argues that a highly inflected language, like the Greek, is superior to an uninflected language because it allows for possibilities of synthesis that are simply beyond the capabilities of lesser languages and lesser minds. Hence politics in the most radical sense of the term—not *mere* politics—is only accessible by means of the superior education offered by the *Bildungs* tradition.

If there was a counter to the enthusiastic aloofness to "mere" politics characteristic of the founders of the *Bildungs* tradition, it was the rationalization of classical philology introduced by the originators of *Altertumswissenschaft*, the scientific study of the ancient world. It is difficult to say when and how this academic draining of idealism from Greek studies happened. It was rather more a shift of emphasis: the enthusiasm of the amateur philologists of the first generation died out and was replaced by the rigorous methods of a new generation, perhaps symbolized by no one more than August Böckh, with his redefinition of philology as the knowledge of what was known.[12] Here, conveniently, was the shift back from the construction of the *self* emphasized by Herder and Humboldt to the construction of *knowledge* emphasized in the Enlightenment conception of language. Böckh, who was appointed to the chair in classical philology at the new university of Berlin in 1815 and who continued to lecture from this chair for over half a century, was the true founder of *Altertumswissenschaft*, the intent of which, put as plainly as possible, was to reconstruct the economic, political, social, and cultural contexts of the ancient world so that its great figures—thinkers like Plato and writers like Aeschylus—could be explained.[13] The growth and success of *Altertumswissenschaft* was immense in the mid-nineteenth century, but for those like Nietzsche who recalled what had motivated the first generation of classical philologists, the success was one in which the genius of the Greeks was systematically drained away by being explained away. It was a pyrrhic victory.

Altertumswissenschaft had obvious political significance.[14] It was apolitical in a way very different from that of the *Bildungs* tradition. Instead of constructing a Greece that was a distant Republic of Letters led by great minds, it lost itself in the near-at-hand, the pursuit and establishment of facts. Where the *Bildungs* tradition threatened to make educated Germans politically ineffective by making them too cultivated, *Altertumswissenschaft* threatened to make educated Germans politically ineffective by denying them all cultivated interpretive vision. *Altertumswissenschaft* simply assumed that all basic problems about Greece had already been solved and that what remained was the technical mopping-up operation of filling in details about economy, polity, society, and cultural mores. It, too, was laden from the outset with serious potential for crippling the political effectiveness of the German-educated classes.

To sum up, the discipline of classical philology was throughout the nineteenth century deeply divided into two opposed camps. The older *Bildungs* tradition was obviously keyed to a hermeneutic approach to the study of Greece, intent upon an understanding of the exemplary achievements of great men. The newer *Altertumswissenschaft* was keyed, in contrast, to an explanation of human behavior in terms of the established facts of politics, society, and economy. The split in the academic discipline of classical philology reiterated a split in Germany itself, between a nation keyed to a romantic and heroic image of itself and a nation determined to industrialize not only the economy but also the German life-world itself. Fueled by this wider, national split, the academic tempest within classical philology would take on a mean spirit in the last decades of the century.

III

Upon completing his doctoral dissertation under Natorp, Gadamer continued working in the Philosophical Seminar at the Marburg University, but he needed a replacement for the retiring Natorp if he was to move purposefully toward his *Habilitation*.[15] This was neither an automatic nor an immediate move, and so uncertain was Gadamer of what he was moving toward that he chose to push in two complementary directions. He continued to read philosophy and to work in the Philosophical Seminar, where in 1923 he heard the first lectures of Natorp's successor, the young Martin Heidegger. Simultaneously, however, Gadamer moved in the direction of becoming a classical philologist, and this brought him into close association with Paul Friedländer, a protege of the great Berlin philologist Ulrich von Wilamowitz-Moellendorff. Gadamer perfected his Greek under Friedländer and in this context became part of a Thursday-evening reading group at the home of the theologian Rudolf Bultmann.

The triangle comprising Heidegger, Friedländer, and Bultmann was immensely important for Gadamer, for all three thinkers were, in their time, academic radicals. Heidegger was about to launch a new movement designed to reshape Western philosophical thinking. Friedländer was part of a dissident philological movement seeking to overturn the positivistic establishment. Bultmann for his part was the leader of a startling movement in the field of New Testament theology that aimed at creating new modes of interpreting the Bible. All three men were bound to have an impact on the young Gadamer's thinking about hermeneutics. Yet there is reason to look more closely at other influences on the shaping of the

young Gadamer's mind. As Gadamer said in a 1983 letter to
the American Richard Bernstein: "As important as Heidegger
and his 1923 *phronesis* interpretations were for me, I was already prepared for it on my own, above all by my earlier reading of Kierkegaard, by the Platonic Socrates, and by the powerful effect of the poet Stefan George on my generation."[16] It
is to Stefan George and his Circle of academic followers that
one turns to gain a deeper perspective on the early Gadamer.

The poet Stefan George and the German academics who
identified themselves with him, known collectively as the
Stefan George Circle, had an influence on the culture of twentieth-century Germany similar to that of Bloomsbury on the
culture of English-speaking countries. Yet where Bloomsbury has been subjected to microscopic scrutiny, the Stefan
George Circle has been all but forgotten.[17] Of the approximately fifty book titles listed under Stefan George in the library of the Germanistic Seminar in Heidelberg, fewer than
five are studies of the cultural politics of the poet and his
Circle.

This is remarkable when one reflects on the cultural origins of Nazism in Germany. For no group expressed more
poignantly the rising cultural despair of the German middle
classes in the period before and immediately after World War
I than did the George Circle, and no group contributed more to
the symbolism of National Socialism than did the Georgians.
They used the *swastika* as their emblem, employed the term
Führer to designate the leader they were seeking, made clear
that the coming leader was to take charge of a new and third
Reich to replace the barren second *Reich*, and, in speaking of
themselves as a *Kult* of followers of the new leader, provided
the outlines of a totalitarian political party. And if this information is thought to be merely coincidental, then it should be
added that Goebbels, Hitler's Propaganda Minister and the
key person in orchestrating the theatrical side of National
Socialism, studied in Heidelberg in the early 1920s and was
influenced there by a key member of the George Circle, Friedrich Gundolf. Goebbels could have written a separate testi-

mony to the influence of the poet Stefan George on his generation, and indeed there are those who maintain that Goebbels's
first novel was just this.

Yet none of this is to say that the Georgians were Nazis.
In fact, they were not, and precisely because they were the
creators of the cultural symbolism of Nazism, they were
among the first to recognize Nazism as a sham. The poet
Stefan George in fact always showed excellent and sound practical political judgment, as, for example, when he warned his
younger followers in 1914 not to interpret the outbreak of
World War I as the hoped-for collapse of the Second *Reich* that
would pave the way for the coming of the new leader. Similarly, in 1933, when Hitler arrived in power, Stefan George
was among the first prominent non-Jewish and non-Marxist
Germans to emigrate from Germany by way of protest. His
last book of poetry may have been entitled *Das Reich*, but he
was not in the least confused by what Hitler was introducing.
In this respect, George's clear thinking contrasts sharply with
that of Heidegger, who in 1933 was an enthusiastic backer of
Hitler's revolution. Finally, the man who carried out the July
20, 1944, plot on Hitler's life, Graf Stauffenberg, was in his
student days one of the last disciples around the poet Stefan
George. So the direct relationship of the Stefan George Circle
with Nazism is one of utter contempt.

Clearly, the cultural meaning of the Stefan George Circle
is difficult to assess in a balanced way. On the one hand, its
members were the most organized and influential expression
of the cultural despair that afflicted the German upper-middle
classes in Gadamer's formative years. In this respect, they are
very much like Bloomsbury in their significance. But where
Bloomsbury's members were primarily engaged in a rejection
of Victorian society's values in favor of a more hedonistic,
more private, ethical norm, this was not the case with the
Georgians. They rejected the values of an industrializing Wilhelmine Germany in favor of a more public set of values. But
it is precisely here that they went wrong, for their idea of what
constitutes the *public* sphere was profoundly questionable.

For example, the ideas of the *Führer*, the *Reich*, and the *Kult* surrounding the leader and organizing the revolution are all political-sounding concepts, but they are not at all public in content. The Georgians expected the leader to be a poet, and indeed this was why Stefan George himself was at the head of the movement and why he, a poet, could write a book with a title like *Das Reich*.[18] The Georgians made it their concern to discover poets and to put them forth as leaders for Germany. Stefan George himself is widely credited with the discovery of Hugo von Hoffmannsthal. Gundolf wrote very influential biographies of Shakespeare and Goethe, and in each case made no secret that these poets captured the spirit of their respective nations. A young member of the George Circle named Hellingrath presided over a rediscovery of the poet Friedrich Hölderlin, saw to it that all of Hölderlin's works were reissued, and hence made a fetish of this poet that reached its high point in Heidegger's academic commentaries. Besides Stefan George, the Circle included other notable German poets, such as Karl Wolfskehl and Max Kommerell, the latter a close friend of Gadamer at Marburg.

Yet for all that, the Georgians were not putting forth a *public* figure when they extolled the virtues of various poets. They were obviously thinking of archaic Greece when they thought of their model of the poet, but a close examination of their characterization of the poets reveals a distinctly modern and very romantic conception of the poet as a lonely genius possessed of wisdom otherwise inaccessible to his contemporaries. It is, furthermore, a wisdom about an alternative world unavailable to modern, industrializing Germans. It is a utopia in which a perfect language, the language of *Dichtung*, or poetry, is spoken. It thus reiterates a long-standing romantic desire to re-create a synchronically perfect language, free of the analytic corruptions of modern society. Not surprisingly, the theory of language associated with Stefan George and the George Circle was a variation on the theme of *l'art pour l'art*. Language, according to this thinking, was not an instrument that existed for the passive expression of something outside of it. Of course it could be made into this, and in modern scientific-industrial society, precisely this had happened. But pure language, according to the Georgians, expresses nothing outside itself. It is action, metaphorically cast. Indeed, so problematic is the word *expression* that it virtually became a pejorative for the Georgians. Any writer who would express anything—be it thinking, ideas, emotions, feelings, or even mere opinions—would be revealing that he was not a true creator. He was rather a servant of something outside of language, a mere conduit, and hence a slave, the opposite of the Nietzschean superman whom the Georgians adored. He clearly was a genius, but hardly a public figure.

IV

The Stefan George Circle traced its intellectual pedigree back through Mallarmé (who early influenced the young George) to Nietzsche, but it is clear that they were also simply re-creating in precious form the thinking and the mood of the first generation of German-language philosophers, the founders of the *Bildungs* tradition. The discovery of Shakespeare was not original with the Georgians but was a repeat of an experience that had taken place first in the 1780s. The emphasis on the form or *Gestalt* of the self that took shape in language was original with Herder rather than with the Georgians, and similarly the notion of a Republic of Letters that took shape in the cultivation of mind rather than in the accumulation of worldly power was first sketched out by Schiller and was only taken over by the Georgians.

But there was a difference between the first generation of German-language philosophers and the Georgians that needs to be isolated. The Prussians of the period from 1780 to 1820 were dissatisfied with the Prussian state but were never really hostile to it. Therefore they could, if need be, work for it and perhaps change it. Humboldt, Goethe, Fichte, and Hegel all had ambivalent attitudes toward Prussia, but the point is that their ambivalence encompassed a positive as well as a negative side and this side enabled them to maintain a constructive relationship to the Prussian state.[19] Not so the Georgians of the Second *Reich.* Although many of them, as Professors, were state functionaries, all of them despised the *Reich* and wished its end. The unexpected but predictable consequence of this cultural despair was that the Georgians forfeited practically all influence over the policies of the German state. They thus entered into a vicious circle in which they defined themselves as outsiders and were taken for outsiders. They were free to theorize as they wished, but more often than not this meant that they were free to be unrestrained in their political criticism because it would have no practical impact.

Every Georgian knew that Shakespeare, Hölderlin, and Goethe were dead and gone and would not return to save Germany from the linguistic morass, the *Gerede,* that was everywhere to be heard. Therefore, the Georgians knew that their real task was not simply to dig up old poets but rather to sketch in as best they could the *Gestalt* of the coming leader. This German term, originally used by Herder in his prize-winning essay on the origin of language, meant for the Georgians something akin to shape or form, and what it introduced was a highly romantic element into Georgian thinking on psychology. For Herder language was not, as I have already noted, simply a flattened mechanism for expressing ideas or feelings. It is rather the mode in which human beings take shape, or rather form their *Gestalt.* There is no consciousness of reality or self-consciousness except in terms of the *Gestalt* it takes in language. Herder's question about the *origin* of language is somewhat misleading if we construe it diachronically. Language is always original, insofar as it is the story of human creation, and hence it has to be grasped synchronically.

At this point, it might be helpful to insert a word about *time* and concepts of time in reference to the language theory.[20]

The so-called timelessness of a play by Shakespeare or a poem by Goethe refers to a reader's experience that is anything but timeless. That is to say, in a play by Shakespeare or a poem by Goethe, all time seems pulled together in an instant that endures because it is memorable and therefore, for the reader, meaningful. Indeed, one might claim that it is memorable because it is meaningful. The quality at work here is a sort of timelessness, and this is the quality of any literature or piece of literature that merits the name classical. What is at work here is a holistic conception of time, and the emphasis is on the harmonic coming together of the so-called past, present, and future. To this experience of a sudden synthesis of time, we might apply the term *synchronic*, taking it from Saussure. The opposite of a holistic or synchronic conception of time is a fragmented or *diachronic* conception, which is the one we are familiar with from clocks and other analytic instruments. This is real time, expressed artificially in our measuring instruments. Here time is flattened out into discrete moments located in the past, present, and putative future. The clock articulates time as a series of measurable (and therefore discrete) moments, and this quality enables us to articulate events or thoughts into sequences. The diachronic conception of time is keyed to positivistic thinking. Indeed, it is one of the conditions of the possibility of positivistic thinking. The Georgians, needless to say, were employing a holistic or synchronic concept of time when they looked to find the *Gestalt* of a great literary figure.

The biographies of Shakespeare, Frederick the Great, Goethe, Nietzsche, George himself, as well as Hellingrath's famous biographical sketch of Hölderlin are writings within a genre called *Gestaltsbiographien*, or *Gestalt*-biographies. To say that this genre did not make a clean separation between fact and fiction is accurate but misleading. What it sought out in the life of a person is precisely the legendary, the mythical, the edifying, the illuminating, all of which are synchronic moments. To use Heidegger's language, it sought out that which had *presence*, and this was never factual in the analytic sense

of the term. A fact is a dismembered piece of the whole—
Stefan George's adjective was *zerstückelt*. The problem with
the focus on facts that dominated *Altertumswissenschaft* is
that the whole came to be forgotten. The reason of course is
deceptively simple: The fact is itself a whole. It is a discrete
spatial or temporal entity that can be understood on its own
terms. The problem that arises is then one of communication
in a world of discrete facts. In reference to an individual life,
what the Georgians were saying when they wrote *Gestaltsbiographien* was that a life is something more than an accumulation of individual facts. There is an organically whole quality
to life which precedes the analytically reduced factual life.
Thus no matter how true all the established facts of academic
Platonic scholarship were, they necessarily missed the point of
Plato's life. It was this that the Georgians were after in their
Gestaltsbiographien.

The first Georgian to apply the concept of *Gestalt* to Plato
was Kurt Hildebrandt, whose introduction to a translation of
the *Symposium* published in 1911 argued that Plato's language was self-sufficient and should be understood in purely
literary terms. Hildebrandt thus cleared the way for another
Georgian, Heinrich Friedemann, to write the first real *Gestalt*-biography of Plato. Friedemann had done his doctoral dissertation in Marburg under Natorp, was deeply influenced by
Friedrich Gundolf (whom he considered a *Führer*), and later
had gone to Berlin where he showed the work on Plato to
Stefan George. In 1914 it was published by Bondi, Stefan
George's personal press, as *Platon: seine Gestalt*.[21] The key to
understanding this book was once again the Natorpian argument that Plato had no doctrine of ideas that he expressed in
language. On the basis of this claim, Friedemann was then
able to argue the subsidiary claim that Plato was a true *Führer* introducing a new *Reich*.

Gadamer met Hildebrandt immediately after the war, in
Natorp's office. He heard of Friedemann from Natorp and may
have read him in this early period. He certainly had read him
by the mid-1920s. In the same period, Gadamer made his first

acquaintance with the poetry of Stefan George, and by his own account he was left thunderstuck by it.[22] But however significant these moments are, they are mere moments and are hence minor when compared to the systematic and prolonged influence exerted by Paul Friedländer, yet another follower of Stefan George who was also Gadamer's professor in Greek philology in Marburg after the war. Friedländer is worth looking at in more detail because he was, unlike Hildebrandt and Friedemann, no outsider to the German academic establishment. Ironically, Friedländer embodied the full force of the contradictions of the German academic world because he was not just a follower of Stefan George but was also a star pupil of Ulrich von Wilamowitz-Moellendorff. Since Wilamowitz embodied everything that the Georgians detested, Friedländer somehow managed to get himself on both sides of one of the leading academic quarrels of the German nineteenth century. It is a spectacle worth describing in detail, but only after grasping the outlines of the German nineteenth-century educational system.

V

When Wilhelm von Humboldt created the Prussian institution of the *Gymnasium*, at the beginning of the nineteenth century, he initiated a curriculum designed to effect a revolution from above.[23] Even the name *Gymnasium* tells us this, for it is not only a Greek term but is also the place where one strips naked and prepares for action. Thus, symbolically at least, the *Gymnasium* was conceived as a sanctuary where Germans were to shed their passive provincialism and, by means of the inflected Greek language, actively construct their true selves. In the same period, around 1810, Humboldt also grasped that the reformed Prussian educational system would all too soon come to grief unless it were capped off by a

university system with an elite of philosophers keyed to producing inspiring books about the Hellenes. Although Humboldt never said as much when he created the University of
Berlin, he probably had in mind the sharp contrast in educational values provided by the universities at Halle and Göttingen. Halle had served as a training ground for Prussian
functionaries of all varieties, and Göttingen had established
itself as a new kind of university which stressed the construction of the spirit. Obviously, Humboldt would have favored the
Göttingen model, but as a Prussian functionary himself, he
would have wanted to have close control over it, and what better way to do this than by setting up a university in Berlin itself. Thus as the intellectual support system for the new Prussian educational system, or rather as the crown of the entire
effort, the University of Berlin was created. From this center,
a classical renaissance was supposed to radiate out over the
spokes of the *Gymnasium* and reform the soul of every Prussian schoolboy.

The legendary beginning of this remarkable rise of classical Greek philology to its nineteenth-century position as the
crown jewel of the German educational system can even be
dated: It occurred, so it was later said, on April 8, 1777, when
Friedrich August Wolf, registering at the University of Göttingen, insisted on being inscribed as *studiosus philologiae*.[24]
The meaning of this act was clear from the outset. German
universities in the eighteenth century were basically voca-
tional schools where one learned an upper-middle-class trade,
like law, medicine, civil engineering, Lutheran theology, or
public administration. Halle, as noted, was the prime example
of this format. But the new emphasis on the creation of the self
through language that had emerged out of Herder's 1772 essay quickly passed over into educational philosophy and from
thence into a program for educational reform. Wolf's symbolic
move in 1777 was the beginning of the reconstruction of the
secondary-school curriculum around a philological core, and
although Göttingen was the legendary birthplace of the new
emphasis on language, Jena soon caught up. But as Jena's ex-

perience demonstrated—Fichte, Schelling, and Hegel all
taught at Jena but soon left, and Humboldt and Schiller made
their home there but also soon left—there was a need to routinize the new beginning. This systematization took place
with the founding of the University of Berlin by Humboldt in
1810, a mere generation after Wolf's initial symbolic act.

Obviously there is a contradiction in this Prussian reception
of Greece that needs to be brought into sharp relief. Whatever
Humboldt's intentions, he was capitalizing on an enthusiasm
for Greece—associated with the names of Wolf, Goethe, Hölderlin, Schiller, and Hegel—that could not be separated from
an enthusiasm for the ideas if not the actual experience of revolution. Yet Humboldt, as a servant of the Prussian state,
could not have intended to institutionalize revolution. He was
rather trying to channel its spirit, and in trying to channel it,
he was undoubtedly trying to control it. But we shall never
know exactly what Humboldt had in mind, and probably he
himself did not know. Like those rare thinkers who have ideas
in private life and then suddenly find themselves in a public
position that provides them the opportunity to institutionalize
their ideas, Humboldt was ambivalent. The creation of the
University of Berlin as the capstone of the entire Prussian educational system was a revolutionary act and, simultaneously, a very conservative act. It brought the spirit of revolution to the very heart of Berlin, but by doing so it also brought
it within easy surveillance of the Prussian police.

The iron discipline of the Prussian *Gymnasium* and the
rapid rise of the nineteenth-century German university into a
rigid bureaucracy of state functionaries were to prove Humboldt correct. The energies associated with Greece could be
put to conservative uses in the service of the Prussian state.
Indeed, no one proved better at this than Hegel, who was at
once the ultimate Prussian professor but was also said to open
a bottle of champagne every July 14. The dark, passionate
Greece that Nietzsche invoked in *Birth of Tragedy* and which
seemed to so many to be acted out in the French Revolution
thus was securely placed within German academic respect-

ability.[25] But ironically, the success of Humboldt's plan for a rebirth of Greece within the iron framework of the Prussian state also carried within itself the seeds of later failure, for Prussia's growing strength made her the model for all Germany, and it was clearly doubtful whether the unification and industrialization of Germany would lead to a simple and unproblematic expansion of the Prussianized Greek spirit.

Unification brought a sternly authoritarian and basically agricultural eastern state together with the more industrializing and urbanizing states of the Rhine area, and the fear was that Prussia, in achieving a political conquest of Germany, had ironically opened herself to cultural conquest. The problem may be put differently and more simply: Industrialization demands that the study of science and the acquisition of analytical skills be put at the core of school and university curriculum. Industrialization further demands that these core curricular elements be treated with the love, honor, and obedience that any centrally located academic discipline demands— in sum, that an industrial culture be created to sustain an industrial civilization. But this kind of routinization, rationalization, and bureaucratization—with its attendant division of labor—was precisely what the legendary Wolf was arguing against with his symbolic move on April 8, 1777. Now Humboldt's hellenophilic core curriculum was conceived to combat precisely these tendencies emerging out of the European Enlightenment, and thus the unification of Germany created a cultural problem that was unavoidable and deeply distressing for any product of the Prussian *Gymnasium*.

Nietzsche was a pupil in the small Prussian city of Schulpforte and a graduate of its *Gymnasium*, unquestionably the best classical *Gymnasium* in nineteenth-century Germany. After university studies, he had begun his career as a classical philologist. Indeed, Nietzsche's early academic career was one of the most brilliantly promising in nineteenth-century Germany. He had done his doctorate very rapidly, habilitated with record speed, and been appointed *Extraordinarius* at twenty-four years old, *Ordinarius* one year later. This was an unheard-of rise in rigid nineteenth-century Germany. Had Nietzsche played his cards right, he could have moved up from his somewhat geographically marginal first professorial position in Basel to the key central position of Berlin *Ordinarius* for *Altphilologie*. Whether Nietzsche ever thought this way, we do not know. We only know that the *Birth of Tragedy* did not fit into the 1872 model of what a preeminent professor of classical philology should be doing. It may have fit the model of a Dionysian revolutionary Greece that Humboldt and his contemporaries had dreamed of, but it did not fit the model of Apollonian rationality that an industrializing Germany was becoming. Nietzsche in sum posed a challenge to the industrial determination of the German academic curriculum that unification promised. In the euphoria of 1871, Nietzsche stood out as a voice from the Prussian past, a hysterical fundamentalist who had to be resisted in the name of the new Second *Reich*.

Let me put this slightly differently and in a somewhat more limited framework. The quarrel over Nietzsche's first book was not so much between a romantic Germany of the past and the industrializing Germany of the future. To contemporaries it was more a quarrel between the vision of philology of the first generation of Prussians, men like Humboldt, Wolf, and Schiller, and the reality of the established *Altertumswissenschaft* of a second generation of men, such as Böckh and Mommsen. The newer *Altertumswissenschaft* was keyed to producing and accumulating facts, the more material the better, and was inclined to take the romantic inspiration for granted. Without ever intending as much, *Altertumswissenschaft* was thus keyed to the mood of an industrializing Germany, also intent on producing and accumulating. Nietzsche, in contrast, was keyed to the mood of a Prussia of the Humboldtian past, which was primarily concerned with the inspirational value of Greece in the *Bildung* of the nascent German nation. The quarrel over Nietzsche's first book was fought out in this context.

The first and for a while the only person to point this out

publicly was another classical philologist from the Prussian town of Schulpforte: Ulrich von Wilamowitz-Moellendorff. Wilamowitz's review was a bitter, unqualified attack that relentlessly pursued and made a mockery of every last detail of Nietzsche's effort.[26] The review was so insulting that it had to be rebutted or otherwise Nietzsche would have conceded his entire academic career. Yet Nietzsche himself did not respond. He rather entrusted this task to a friend, thereby inviting a broadening of the conflict. The rebuttal was produced by Erwin Rohde, yet another young scholar who would also become, with time, a leading and well-known classical philologist, the author of an excellent book called *Psyche*.[27] But Rohde's defense of Nietzsche—called *Afterphilologie!*—did not put an end to things.[28] Wilamowitz only responded with a stepped-up counterattack called *Mehr Zukunftsphilologie!*[29] ("More Future Philology!"), and now he included Rohde as an object of his attack and, by implication, the entire first-generation tradition that they represented.

In the curious way these things work, the event was also the beginning of Wilamowitz's own brilliantly successful rise to the top of the German academic world. While Nietzsche slipped quietly out of academic life and into temporary obscurity, Wilamowitz rose to professorial position and eventually became no less than the Berlin *Ordinarius*. He thus enraged his opponents by arriving at the center of the old Prussian educational system. He there and then used his great influence to advocate a view of classical philology that was abhorrent to the one that Nietzsche had represented. Where Nietzsche had implicitly claimed that the philologist's task was to capture the real revolutionary spirit of Greece, its soul and its genius, Wilamowitz believed that the classical philologist was involved in a mere mopping-up operation, and he virtually said as much. To the delight of his many enemies, Wilamowitz repeatedly claimed that the only thing he had to teach was *method*, thereby confirming the suspicion that he was at the center of the putative industrialization of German cultural life.[30] Furthermore, Wilamowitz made it no secret that he meant method to be applied to obscure text materials that had not yet been reconstructed. Basically, Wilamowitz believed that the writings of great thinkers like Plato or Aristotle should not be repeatedly reworked because we already knew what they thought, a thesis which outraged those Germans who believed that the creative potential of a great thinker is never exhausted. For Wilamowitz, the classical philologist should fully concentrate on marginal figures so as to provide a complete picture of Greece. In sum, where Nietzsche had been a spirited revolutionary in providing thought-provoking interpretations of great Greeks like Aeschylus, Homer, Socrates, and Plato, Wilamowitz was an unabashed *Altertumswissenschaftler* who believed in producing and accumulating cleaned-up empirical materials from which induction could proceed. Nietzsche represented the old Prussia into which Humboldt had injected the revolutionary spirit of Greece, Wilamowitz the new Germany of the industrialists of the Ruhr Valley.

It should be obvious by now that Wilamowitz was also in conflict with the spirit of the Stefan George Circle. As a group, the Circle did not take shape until the first decade of the twentieth century, and they did not immediately have a consciousness of the implications of *Gestaltsbiographie* for the quarrel that was going on among classical philologists. But soon enough they did recognize that what Nietzsche was doing in *Birth of Tragedy* was a *Gestaltsbiographie* of Aeschylus, and that Wilamowitz's continuing opposition to this genre made him their enemy. They thus began publicly to attack Wilamowitz, and recognizing that Wilamowitz would leave out nothing in his counterattacks, they made certain that their first attacks were as vicious as they could make them. Stefan George himself attacked Wilamowitz, and Wilamowitz went so far as to get the University of Berlin to cancel a scheduled and festive appearance by the poet himself in 1910. For a group of academics such as the early Stefan George Circle, this was perceived as a crushing defeat and a stinging reminder of how powerful Wilamowitz was.

The point, to be as brief and circumspect as possible, is that by 1910 the positivistic *Altertumswissenschaften* had won out seemingly decisively over the *Bildungs* tradition. Yet on the other side, however unoriginal and outrageously romantic the Stefan George Circle might appear to be, they were putting up a remarkably good fight against positivism.[31] People were listening. Hence the years shortly before 1914 record a striking irony: Positivism was at the height of its power in the academic world, but it did not follow from this that the speculative opposition was at its nadir. It too was increasing its influence. Hence the famous quarrel between Nietzsche and Wilamowitz was far from over in the first decades of the twentieth century. In almost all respects, it was more heated in 1910–14 than it had been forty years earlier.

VI

In 1918, as the Second *Reich* began to show unambiguous signs that its end was very near, so too did Wilamowitz. In that desperate year the Berlin *Ordinarius* completed a long-awaited major book called *Platon*.[32] It was not a response to the Georgians, who after all were a minor thorn in Wilamowitz's side. It was rather a comprehensive statement of Wilamowitz's lifetime of thought and scholarship about Plato, and hence it was designed to be above petty academic quarrels. Yet for all that, this book showed far more than its author ever intended. It was not, as far as I know, attacked by anyone from the Stefan George Circle. In fact, from all sides it was met with an embarrassed silence or with respectful but vague praise for the great scholar's entire career, the academic reviewer's curious way of drawing attention away from the near-at-hand.

The reason for this had less to do with Wilamowitz personally than with Germany's changed circumstances in 1918. Wilamowitz's *Platon* was flat in its language, yet it was more than a rehash of familiar and established opinions on Plato. It was in fact a first-rate piece of *Altertumswissenschaft*. It might have been construed as a final statement of Wilamowitz's long-standing claim that although there was little more to say about the so-called great thinkers, a good deal could be said about their contexts, and from this point of view, a good deal could be said about them. But this was not what was wanted in the Germany of 1918. Wilamowitz was faltering at precisely a time where leadership was most needed. Germany was nearing defeat on the battlefield, and the least far-sighted German knew that this would mean revolution at home. What was sought in 1918 was a Plato who would address himself to the changes that were needed in Germany, a Plato who would recognize the cultural crisis and would respond to it with concrete arguments for change at the deepest levels of the German *Geist*. Precisely the kind of writing Max Weber was to do in 1918 and 1919, Wilamowitz was unable to do in 1917. Wilamowitz pretended to be aloof from the dirty political realities of 1918, but his readers were not. He was the unpolitical German, but at precisely this moment the educated German public was ceasing to be quite so unpolitical.

It is said that Wilamowitz's *Platon* was the beginning of the end for Wilamowitz. Behind his back, a movement began to ease him out of the Berlin chair for *Altphilologie*, and the movement was not simply an expression of the career ambitions of younger men but was more so a reflection of the need for spirited leadership at the center of the German educational system, a conclusion which was shared not just by academics but also by key people in the Ministry of Education. Wilamowitz retired in proper form in 1919, but there is no indication that he sought this retirement. There is rather every reason to believe that the University and the Ministry used every civilized means at its disposal to coax Wilamowitz into this decision.

The identity of Wilamowitz's successor had been obvious for years. He was Werner Jaeger, who had been Professor at Kiel since 1912 and had also established himself as having a way of looking at Greek philosophy that differed from Wilamowitz's.

Jaeger was the obvious choice for this position at this time for two reasons. He was first of all an established and respected philologist, one of the best in Germany. What should be emphasized is that on academic grounds alone Jaeger might still have been chosen to be Wilamowitz's successor. But what made Jaeger the obvious choice was that he was also a forceful and attractive politician.[33] Thus on this second ground, taken alone, he might have been chosen for the position of Berlin *Ordinarius*, even if he had been a second-rate philologist, which he was not. The fact that Jaeger put together academic and political qualifications made him the obvious choice for the position.

Jaeger was by no means a Georgian, but he was nonetheless a humanist who believed that philology could not be conducted according to the naive positivistic method practiced by Wilamowitz and the conventional *Altertumswissenschaftler*. Jaeger had rather been impressed by the work of Hermann Usener, a great philologist, already admired by Nietzsche when Usener was at Leipzig, before he moved on to become the Berlin *Ordinarius*.[34] Usener had married Lily Dilthey, the sister of the Berlin philosopher Wilhelm Dilthey, and thereby had come under the influence of Dilthey's *life* philosophy. Indeed Usener became Dilthey's leading follower in his lifetime. He believed that *life* was the basic category of academic scholarship, and that it could be used in classical philology as an organizing tool for the basic categories of *Altertumswissenschaft*. Usener's thinking thus promised to restore the wholeness of life that had been destroyed in the analytic approach of *Altertumswissenschaft*.

Usener's life philosophy could also be used to address knotty everyday problems like the dating of manuscripts, and this is what Jaeger did in his famous 1923 biography called *Aristotle*.[35] He conceived of Aristotle's life as a whole that went through certain necessary stages, beginning with Platonic idealism and culminating in Aristotelian realism. He also conceived of Greek civilization itself as conforming to life categories, and hence all Greek thought in Jaeger's eyes was a movement from poetic idealism to analytic realism. Jaeger would later employ this enlarged concept of life in writing his multivolume *Paideia*,[36] but in the 1920s he became the center of a storm of controversy for his *Aristotle*.[37]

Jaegar did not consider all of Aristotle. He was only interested in the ethics, and given Jaeger's active political career, it seems only reasonable to say that *his* Aristotle was remarkably well keyed to *his* political program for the reform of education and society in Weimar Germany, a program which he called the *Third Humanism*. The problem with this program was that Jaeger's Aristotle seemed to be a reincarnation of a nineteenth-century German *Altertumswissenschaftler:* He took a distinctly positivistic approach to the making of his system of ethics. Jaeger's Aristotle began with the idealism of Plato and thus in the opening stages of intellectual life corresponded, however roughly, to the idealistic first generation of German philologists, honest but immature philhellenes like Humboldt and Hölderlin. Jaeger's Aristotle then outgrew Platonic idealism and became a realist, thus roughly moving along the same path by which more scientific thinkers like Böckh created *Altertumswissenschaft*. If one were not blinded by the admitted brilliance of Jaeger's philology, one might easily miss the conservative political message that gave the philology its thrust and its structure: Greece was still the model for Germany, but it was hardly the Greece of Hölderlin, Humboldt, or Nietzsche. It was rather the Greece of Böckh, Wilamowitz, and now Jaeger. This was a Greece which was not irrational and revolutionary but was rather reasonable, positivistic, and thoroughly rational in the construction of ethical and political life. It was a thoroughly *a*political Greece.

In the characteristic fashion of *Altertumswissenschaft*, Jaeger based his scholarship upon a grasp of time that was thoroughly positivistic. By this I mean that Jaeger flattened human life by addressing it in terms of sequentially ordered categories. This enabled him to date manuscripts, and while there is no doubt that his achievement is brilliant, it is also questionable as a way of reconstructing genuinely original thinking. The problem is that it employs a diachronic conception of time, that is to say, a sense in which time is flattened so that a measuring rod may be provided for establishing facts. This may lead to impressive scholarly achievements along the lines of *Altertumswissenschaft*, but such a diachronic arrangement is deadly to the possibility of producing a *Gestalt*-biography. Events of a life become mere facts, preceded and succeeded by other facts. The danger of this conception is that when applied to mind it will cause us to miss what is most important, namely, the synchronic character of any thought that is worth reflecting on.

The significance of Werner Jaeger for the emergence of the point of view of the early writings of Hans-Georg Gadamer will become apparent in chapter 3. Jaeger is an ambivalent figure. On the one hand, he represents a break with the tradition of *Altertumswissenschaft*. His clear intent is to return to the *Bildungs* tradition of the first generation of German classical philologists. Yet simultaneously, he is a prisoner of his own superb training: Even with the adoption of Usener's life categories, he still is prone to organize the life of a great thinker into factual segments, and this adds up to a *flattening* of the life of the great thinker. Jaeger never intended to write a *Gestalt*-biography of Aristotle, but on the other hand, he also did not intend Aristotle's life to become a mere sequence of illustrations of a larger historical process that determined that life. Yet the latter is what Jaeger's achievement in his *Aristotle* added up to. It therefore became Jaeger's fate to provide a perfect foil for what the young Gadamer wanted to say: He was an *Altertumswissenschaftler* who had almost, but not quite, made it back to the first principles of the founders of German classical philology.

VII

Jaeger's succession to the Berlin chair is only one aspect of the decline of the *Altertumswissenschaft* represented by Wilamowitz. Another aspect, and a more telling one for the formation of Gadamer's career, was the defection of another star pupil of Wilamowitz, namely, Paul Friedländer. There was never any real chance that Friedländer could have succeeded to the key Berlin chair. As a scholar and a personality he was never the equal of Jaeger, and in addition he was a Jew at a time when Jews were allowed into some academic positions, usually *Extraordinarien*, but most certainly not into the chairs and never into the key Berlin chair. When Friedländer left the army at the end of the war, he thus did not head back to Berlin but instead went to Marburg to take up a position there as a professor of classical philology. It was from this place that his defection took place in 1922.

In that year, Friedländer wrote Wilamowitz a long letter, more than twenty pages in handscript.[38] He outlined the reasons for his defection, and perhaps inevitably the letter was a manifesto of a new approach to Plato. Friedländer addressed Wilamowitz as "Master," a form of deference that was still common in German academic life but in the circumstances of this letter was bound to come across in an ironically painful manner. Friedländer recounted his experience in the trenches of the eastern front and made clear that the war had helped him reevaluate his relationship to classical philology. He had come to value Plato more highly as a great and original thinker. As a result, Friedländer came to view himself differently. Friedländer had obviously gone through a *Bildungs* process, and he had arrived at a new level of *Selbstbewusstsein,* or self-consciousness.

Friedländer wrote that he no longer considered himself a mere laborer on the margins of classical literary tradition. He no longer wanted to do the kind of mopping-up operations that distinguished Wilamowitz's approach to classical philology. This was a clear rebuff to Wilamowitz, who had always emphasized *Altertumswissenschaft*'s emphasis on context and deemphasized the great figures of Greece. But then Friedländer went on to mete out what had to be received as an even sharper rebuff: He argued that upon reflection he agreed with Nietzsche and Stefan George in their appreciation of the

Greeks, and he could only mean by this that he was doing a complete about-face from Wilamowitz's approach to classical philology. A few sentences of Friedländer's long letter to Wilamowitz suggest its flavor and are hence worth quoting:

> In recent years I have been pained by an uncertainty in my relationship to you, something I did not feel earlier. I am in opposition to you in many things that are important, struggle against you in my inner being and have the feeling that you do not quite dismiss me but nonetheless look at me with disapproval. I have to go back to the past. You were for me in my youth the decisive person, an important aspect of my fate because you were by far the strongest of persons and simultaneously generous and helpful as no other. . . . Since then I have come a long way. Much of the best that I have comes from you. But what I have now become—and this is my other side—I have become in a struggle against you or, perhaps better, against the Wilamowitz in me. Had I earlier not given myself over to you so strongly, the solution now would not have become so painful. . . . If I were to name the names that brought about this reversal, they are . . . Nietzsche, who since my youth has gradually determined with urgency my comprehensive view of life and who especially helped me to form my view of what is *historical.* . . . And in recent years it has been [Stefan] George who has brought on the greatest shock and the strongest rearrangement of all forces. With that you have a brief sketch of my way and you will understand what I earlier called the struggle against the Wilamowitz in me.

Clearly, if this much could be said, the long hegemony of Ulrich von Wilamowitz-Moellendorff was at an end. Friedländer was torn because as a person Wilamowitz was very generous but as a scholar represented an ideal that was impossible for the postwar generation. The *Wilamowitz in me* to

which Friedländer refers is the nineteenth-century positivistic model of classical philology propounded originally by the
later Böckh. It was against this dehumanized conception that
Friedländer was rebelling, and the rebellion was carried out
in the name of Nietzsche and Stefan George because they had
always represented the alternative. Friedländer intimates in
this letter what that alternative was when he stresses such
terms as Nietzsche's vision of the *historical*, by which Friedländer meant a holistic or, as I have called it in this chapter, a
synchronic approach to the portrayal of past events.[39]

Let me sum up before concluding this chapter. Throughout I
have been trying to emphasize, from varying points of view,
that German classical philology in the nineteenth century was
torn between two conflicting points of view. The first was that
of the founding fathers of German classical philology—men
like Wolf, Humboldt, and Schleiermacher—and it emphasized
that the redeeming purpose of classical studies was to capture
the heroic spirit of ancient Greece and convey this through
Bildung to new generations of German students. These men—
along with Nietzsche, Natorp, and the academic philologists of
the Stefan George Circle—wanted to spark a revolution of the
spirit in the soul of those few Germans who were capable of
such a revolution. Against this minority there was, increasingly as the nineteenth century wore on and Germany grew
prosperous through unity and industrialization, a tendency to
routinize classical philology and insist that it perform as any
other disciplined academic study. The men who insisted in going in this direction came to be known as *Altertumswissenschaftler*, and what was held against them was their materialism and positivism. Although this movement started under
August Böckh, it reached its positivistic zenith in the person
and the work of Ulrich von Wilamowitz-Moellendorff. The
Altertumswissenschaftler were in some sense symbolic of the
spirit of Wilhelm's Second *Reich*, and with the collapse of that
Reich in World War I, the way was opened—at long last, the
Nietzscheans and Georgians would say—for a serious bid to
return to the revolutionary spirit of the founders of classical

philology. Although Paul Friedländer was a minor figure in this movement, he was Gadamer's teacher, and hence he represents a key link in a chain of events that leads up from Humboldt through Nietzsche and the Stefan George Circle to Gadamer's early writings.

We do better to turn from Friedländer directly to his student Gadamer to get an even fuller answer to what the influence of Stefan George was on the early Weimar generation. In 1983, Gadamer delivered a paper in Heidelberg on the "Influence of Stefan George on Scholarship."[40] One of the things he did in this paper was to define precisely the same term to which Friedländer referred. What Stefan George gave to the young Gadamer was a clear sense that the *historical* was above all a sensitivity for the unique in all that is transmitted to us from the past. The historical in this sense was contrasted to historicism, which was identified by Gadamer as the attempt to subsume the individual under larger impersonal categories. The historical school of the German nineteenth century in effect deindividualized the individual with its diachronic conception of time, while the advocates of a holistic or synchronic grasp of time sought to restore uniqueness. The reason for this was to enable the past to really speak to us. If we subsume everything into diachronic categories with which we are already comfortable, then the past cannot speak to us, and conversation is impossible. It is only when the past regains its authentic voice that a key condition of conversation is created. It was in respect to this sense of the really unique in the past, Gadamer notes, that he introduced the term *fusion of horizons*.

What becomes clear upon a careful reading of Gadamer's recollection of the influence of Stefan George on the sciences is that the *Dichter* George brought a holistic vision of a very special kind to an area that tended to be flattened out by what George, according to Gadamer, called *mechanical thinking*. For example, Gadamer notes, George makes a typographical distinction between *Ich* and *ich*, both of which mean *I* in English. What Stefan George wants to say is that the ego, the *I* writ large, can be holistically restored only by bringing it into conversation. In *Jahr der Seele*, Stefan George warned against the notion of biography as a record of the establishment of the seemingly autonomous Ego. What really stands behind the supposedly autonomous *Ich* (the *I* writ large) is a conversation between the *ich* (the *I* writ small) and the *du* (the intimate form of you). Once the *I* and the *thou* are restored as conversational partners, what becomes clear is that they share the same soul. So what Stefan George is getting at, according to Gadamer, is that soul is a universal, a holistic thing that we can get back to if we overcome the subject/object dichotomy characteristic of the modern period.

It pays to pause for just a moment to capture the meaning of this thought. The German terms for "you" are a familiar and communal *du* and a distant and societal *Sie*. In these two words, *Gemeinschaft*, or community, is set against *Gesellschaft*, or society. Gadamer, following this line of reasoning, then makes an artificial distinction between the *ich* and the *Ich* that corresponds to this other distinction. He then assigns to the poetry of Stefan George the demand for a return from modern societal formalization—the artificial relationship between the *Sie* and the *Ich*—to a real conversation between the *du* and the *ich*. What Gadamer drew from George was precisely the same impetus that led Nietzsche, Natorp, and Friedländer to seek to return from the positivism of *Altertumswissenschaft* to the real revolutionary possibilities of Humboldtian classical philology, the *Bildungs* tradition.

For Gadamer what was important was the sound, not the sight, of George's poetry, and if I understand Gadamer correctly here, what is being emphasized is the mythological quality of George's words. "Myth," says Gadamer, "is something that one must listen to [*hören*] and in respect to which one cannot do justice except as a hearer [*ein Horchender*] and as one who obeys [*gehorchend*]." Every German speaker in Gadamer's audience would have heard the play of words in this sentence and would have understood that George's and Gadamer's reason for rediscovering the importance of the sound of language had to do with the lost wholeness of the

word. Gadamer repeats this thought in different form a few
pages later. He argues that in poetry, " . . . language is not
only a bearer of meaning, so that one takes from it something
like a piece of information. It is rather also that into which one
enters and dwells." Language can, Gadamer notes, be like a
ritual. With ritual nothing is taken note of, but one is simply
taken in by the poetry of it. Gadamer criticizes Protestants
who claim that the saying of the rosary by Catholics is mindless because the words are simply mumbled without being understood. His point is that there is nothing to know, that what
is foremost in the rosary is the ritual itself, and it is for that
reason that it endures. "The word," Gadamer concludes, "is
not a mere bearer of meaning."

Thoughts like these were essential to the members of the
Stefan George Circle. Their theory of language always emphasized that language did not *express* anything outside of it. At
its best, language was an expression of nothing more than the
play of words in the language, and one therefore had to refocus
one's awareness of wordplay in distinction to the presupposed
feelings, emotions, or thoughts that language was supposedly
expressing. Let me note once again something that Gadamer
is not mentioning in his 1983 lecture. The thought that language does not express anything outside itself is basic to the
reinterpretation of Plato as a *Dichter* rather than a philosopher. The thought sounds absurd on the face of it, but all it
means is that Plato does not have a doctrine of ideas that he
expresses in his language. All he has is the wordplay of his dialogues, and a right understanding of Plato the *Dichter* can
only be gained by listening to these dialogues. As Gadamer
learned from Natorp, it is the Platonic myths that really count
in Plato, and these are not ideas.

Finally in the lecture on Stefan George, Gadamer turns to
Plato and acknowledges the influence of the Stefan George
Circle on the modern German reception of the great Greek
thinkers. He mentions Hildebrandt and Friedemann, and he
notes also the influence of thinkers influenced by Stefan
George who published their Plato books in the 1920s,

specifically Friedländer, Singer, and Reinhardt. Gadamer in the 1983 paper manages all of these acknowledgments under the rubric of what he calls *The New Plato Picture*, and he then goes on to identify what was essential to this picture.

The new Plato picture has to do with what actually happens in the didactic conversations that take place between Socrates and his interlocutors, and this happening must be understood if one is to come to the correct understanding (*das rechte Verständnis*) of Plato. What happens is a revelation of the inner relationship between that which is thought and that which one is. In Gadamer's words: "Socratic-Platonic dialogue-logic is constructed on the basis of a doric harmony between *Logos* and *Ergon*." Gadamer explains this as follows: Not everyone is capable of every insight, and therefore someone who simply repeats a true proposition without realizing it reveals his lack of insight insofar as he cannot defend the proposition. "Thereupon rests Socratic dialogue: it is a test not only of propositions but also of souls." Clearly, the thought Gadamer is here returning to and further elaborating is that of the real possibility of conversation between the *du* and the *ich*. What he drew from the academic Georgians was this emphasis, and of course what is being emphasized is *Bildung* in the form of an integral relationship between the knowledge and the soul. Knowledge cannot be separated out from spirit, as is done by those who hold that Plato had a doctrine of ideas that is expressed in his language. What I am and what I know are integrally related.

This then is the *new Plato picture*. It represents the dissolution of a positivistically conceived monological thinker who expresses a doctrine of ideas into a holistic or synchronically conceived dialogical thinker who records in wordplay the conversation between the restored *ich* and the counterpoised *du*. This is the picture that feeds into Gadamer's habilitation thesis, so nicely called *Platos dialektische Ethik*. Gadamer's thesis, stated in his very first sentence, is very simple. He does not mean to argue that Plato's ethics are dialectical. He rather will argue that Plato's dialectics are ethical. He means, we can now say, that it is in conversation between the restored *ich* and the *du* that we reattain the ethical life. There are no ethical principles outside the realm of language that language expresses. Rather, the ethical life is always already within the dialectical play of language. This is the *new Plato picture*.

3

The Initial Challenge
to
Altertumswissenschaft

I

The Germany and the Central Europe of Gadamer's youth were perceived by its more sensitive observers to be something like an inscription, or what Gadamer calls a *writing* culture. Kafka as well as Dostoyevski (who was very popular in pre-war Germany), Musil, and Thomas and Heinrich Mann describe typical Central European scenes in which characters talk like written books. The underground man (who is actually accused of sounding like a book when he speaks), Kafka's "K," Musil's man-without-qualities, and Aschenbach from Thomas Mann's *Death in Venice*, as well as Diederich Hessling from Heinrich Mann's *Der Untertan*, are rigid characters who reveal in their hard and precise speech the frozen quality of their intellectual lives. The inner self they reveal in speech is not really lively. Indeed, in all of the mentioned cases, the inner self is not different at all from the outer self. The inner self is rather a product of socially established values.

If intellectual culture was this way, so too was the Central European state and the political culture that sustained it in the years before World War I. Indeed, in all of the authors mentioned above, the state is always hovering in the background, as a kind of presence that takes final shape in the individual character of an inspector or bureaucrat or middle-level official of some type. The pre–World War Central European state had rapidly evolved from its absolutist beginnings into a huge bureaucracy of functionaries who expressed themselves in written directives, proclamations, declarations, rules, and complex and simple signs hung on post office walls and railroad stations throughout Central Europe. Similarly (because it was nothing more than the outer level of the Central European state), the academic world placed no less decisive an emphasis on published writing. The German university of the time, where professors were paid state employees with a strong allegiance to the state, clearly favored the publicist and had no place for a thinker who could not keep pace with the dominant written academic culture. Such a writing culture rapidly came to be seen as an iron cage from which, for writers like Kafka and academics like Buber, there was no escape.

After the shock of defeat in World War I and the catastrophe of 1918, the thought was bound to occur not merely to isolated intellectuals like the young Heidegger but to artists like Kurt Schwitters and even students like Karl Löwith and Hans-Georg Gadamer that they lived in a world stood upside down. The natural, preferred, and more humane order of things was one in which human beings "dwell" in *speaking* cultures. This is not to say that there would be no writing but rather that writing was not the primordial human activity. Speaking was primordial, and the order of the day was to retrieve it.

In the minds of the first visionaries of a *speaking* culture, the domination of writing had to be broken. Schwitters did this in very literal fashion by breaking words, trolley tickets, and public proclamations in half. His *Merz* art is named for the second half of the German word *Kommerz*. Heidegger attempted to break the established framework of established academic writing by means of an unorthodox writing style. But even before he wrote *Being and Time*, with its spoken style, he made his reputation as a teacher by means of word-of-mouth and on the basis of what he spoke in the lecture hall. Freud wrote immense amounts, but there was no question that a microscopic *speaking* culture involving patient and analyst was absolutely basic to his effort to establish the new science of psychoanalysis. Stefan George for his part placed decisive emphasis on the *spoken* poem, and hence his readings rather than his writings were the decisive moments of his life. Indeed, when the Georgians wrote, it was with a new calligraphy that deprivileged the German noun and emphasized the easy flow of uncapitalized words. All of these artists, writers, and thinkers represented the primordial mood of Weimar Germany. In their work, they were keyed to breaking down the *writing* culture and thereby freeing up the powers of the *spoken* word.

The shift is nowhere better illustrated than in the reinterpretation of Dostoyevski that took shape in the Weimar period. In 1923 Otto Kaus published *Dostojewski und sein Schicksal* and argued that Dostoyevski's novels were basically dialogical and hence not traceable back to a monological point of view.[1] Kaus thus fully anticipated the argument of Mikhail Bakhtin, but what makes Kaus especially interesting is that he explained why Dostoyevski's works were dialogical in terms of a social framework that was in transition from a traditional form to a modern, specifically urban format in which characters with different monological points of view were brought together. In other words, what Kaus shows is that values depend upon a monological social framework. With the breakdown of that framework, or rather with the breakdown of traditional society, a real dialogue ensues, and the often hidden subject of this dialogue are social values.

What I am trying to sketch here is a very different sort of background to the kind of classical philology Gadamer would undertake. I am not describing anything so sharply defined as a paradigm shift in the German intellectual community. I am rather describing a mood, or better, a set of attitudes that were, if anything, all the more powerful as determinants precisely because they were not sharply etched. What I am suggesting is that the defeat of Germany in World War I brought about a mood shift, and this mood shift was bound to lead to a reevaluation of the nineteenth-century German appropriation of Greece. Sigfried Kaehler's reinterpretation of Humboldt is as much a part of this mood shift as is Kaus's novel interpretation of Dostoyevski, and it reminds us that this mood shift had a direct bearing on German political thinking. The Weimar period could hardly avoid a mood shift away from the "eastern" liberalism of Hegel, with its emphasis on the state, to a more "western" type of liberalism, with a decisive emphasis placed on the autonomy of the creative, "speaking" individual and a new found desire to place limits on the institutions of "written" culture, above all the state. Gadamer did not simply plunge into this specific context with a full-blown body of thinking about modernization, but he did enter it in appropriate fashion by framing his first published professional thoughts in terms of the fashionable conflict between *writing* and *speaking* cultures.

II

There are few better ways to begin a German academic career than by picking the right quarrel with a respected and established scholar. If the young Dozent is lucky, the great scholar will respond, and the Dozent will suddenly find himself thrust into the coveted academic limelight. The unknown Wilamowitz began his career in 1871 with just such an attack on Nietzsche, and the young Kurt Hildebrandt, his with a 1910 attack on the then fully established Wilamowitz. In 1927 it was Gadamer's turn, and he chose in his first paper to launch and carry out a polite and respectful but nonetheless incisive attack on Wilamowitz's successor in the Berlin chair, Werner Jaeger.

Unlike the earlier career beginnings of Wilamowitz and Hildebrandt, there was no biting, personal sarcasm to Gadamer's piece, and so consequently he did not generate the personal counterattack that inevitably follows when oversized academic egos are bruised by upstarts. In this respect, Gadamer's first publication was a failure, but in another, more important respect it was a success. It presented a subtle and surprising argument to the effect that Jaeger did not understand the nature of *language* and its impact on philosophy.

In the next two sections I shall be analyzing this first publication. It is a 1927 piece called in German, *"Der aristotelsche PROTREPTIKOS und die entwicklungsgeschichtliche Betrachtung der aristotelischen Ethik."*[2] Loosely translated, the title would read, "Aristotle's PROTREPTICOS and the Developmental-Historical Mode of Looking at Aristotle's Ethics." The quarrel is over an obscure and early Aristotelian text, more specifically, how that text relates to Aristotle's two other and more famous texts on ethics: the *Eudemian Ethics* and the *Nicomachean Ethics*. In the context of this rarified academic question, Gadamer was able to develop his first thoughts on language in its relation to culture.

In his 1923 book called *Aristotle*, Jaeger had argued that there was an internal logic to Aristotle's philosophical thinking which, if used as a standard of measurement, would allow the philologist to date Aristotle's texts on ethics.[3] Jaeger argued that Aristotle was initially a Platonic thinker and that his *Protreptikos* demonstrated this because it adhered to the Platonic doctrine of ideas and closely resembled the late Platonic text called the *Philebos*.[4] The mature Aristotle was represented by the *Nichomachean Ethics*, and this text established the science of ethics because it articulated concepts that were fully related to practical worldly activity. Now between these two Aristotelian texts came the *Eudemian Ethics*, and Jaeger argued that he could locate this text with certainty because of its level of conceptual development. It was not so far away from the Platonic doctrine of ideas as the *Nichomachean Ethics*, but it was not so close as the *Protreptikos*.

Gadamer's quarrel was not so much with Jaeger's philological achievement as with his grasp of Platonic philosophy. To argue, as Jaeger did, that the *Protreptikos* of Aristotle is closely related to the *Philebos* of Plato is correct as far as it goes, but to argue that both correlate because they are centered on the Platonic doctrine of ideas, as that formulation is conventionally understood in philosophical circles, is to make a questionable move in respect to Platonic thinking. To ascribe a doctrine of ideas to Plato was Jaeger's way of projecting a modern and established German academic convention on Plato, and Gadamer would not participate in this. But how was Gadamer to demonstrate that his own position, which still followed Natorp's, was more plausible than Jaeger's?

The title of Gadamer's most famous book, *Truth and Method*, seems to suggest a fundamental distinction. Gadamer has sometimes declared that it does not suggest this, that *truth* is in no inevitable conflict with *method*. What Gadamer's first publication suggests is that the distinction between *truth* and *method* is not basic but is rather derived from a logically prior distinction between a *speaking* and a *writing* culture. At least with the concept of method, this is expressly the case in Gadamer's first publication, for a writing culture needs a method to get at its fixed universal inscribed truths. A speaking culture, in contrast, claims no prior truths. That, indeed, is precisely why it is a *speaking* culture. Implicitly, truth for it is something to be created in dialogue. So what this first writing suggests is that a distinction between speaking and writing cultures is basic to Gadamer's work. Let me now try to better locate this distinction in reference to the actual argument of Gadamer's first academic publication.

According to Gadamer, the "meaning-context" (*Sachzusammenhang*) of classical Greece was one in which practical thinking as well as theoretical thinking was a mode of being of *Nous*, the divine spark that is still in human beings.[5] This is a difficult thought, so it helps to put it more plainly. *Nous* means *mind*, and specific forms of thinking like practical thinking or theoretical thinking are expressions of mind. Together, these forms of mind describe the meaning-context of classical Greece. That is to say, we think in order to produce meaning. Thinking has to have a purpose. The fact that we do it at all, the fact that we are always thinking, the fact that thinking is always troubled—these self-evident facts of thinking strongly suggest that meaning for human beings is not prescribed. For ordinary animals, still in the state of nature, meaning is inscribed and hence prescribed. In a word, meaning is *written*. It is prior to action, and hence action does not require mind. It can be done, as we say, instinctively. But this is not the case for the human animal.

It is in this context of ascribing to man a divine capacity to reason that Plato's supposed doctrine of ideas must be set. The Platonic doctrine of ideas is only, according to Gadamer, a ". . . special philosophical foundation" of what was everywhere the case in a "*speaking* civilization."[6] So right at the outset of his argument against Jaeger, we find Gadamer denying that Plato has a conventional doctrine of ideas; all that Plato is claiming is that man can reason, and this is equivalent to the claim that man can speak intelligently, and the reason for speaking intelligently is that normative answers, values, are not written into our souls or our genes.

Earlier I argued that the distinction between a *writing* culture and a *speaking* culture was helpful in understanding the quality of life in Central Europe both before and after the war. Now the point can be sharpened. The same distinction is helpful for understanding philosophy in general, or German philosophizing in the 1920s, or Platonic philosophy in particular. Philosophy in a *writing* culture will tend to privilege the *answer* rather than the question. It will presuppose an answer that has been given—for example, a set of ideas that predate human beings—and then it will offer a method for uncovering or revealing or discovering the answer. Philosophy in a *speaking* culture, in contrast, privileges the *question* rather than the answer. The Ten Commandments, for example, are writ-

ten answers to forgotten or repressed questions, and they function as foundations to a writing culture, one that is quite literally based on the written book. Similarly, the laws of Solon are
written answers to live problems which acted out social questions, and they worked to establish a writing culture, one that
presumably developed a method for passing from generation
to generation the meaning of Solon's laws.

There is no end to the examples of *writing* cultures. For example, American civilization with its emphasis on a *written*
constitution. The problem is to find good examples of *speaking*
cultures. Classical Greece, at least Gadamer's construction of
it, is one of these. Like Hannah Arendt's vision of workers'
councils, the classical *polis* of the early Gadamer's imagination is a speaking culture. It privileges the question because it
is aware, at however subconscious a level, of its *situatedness*,
which is nothing more than a different way of saying that the
polis had an awareness that it did not possess definitive answers to the most troubling problems of human relations. The
vision here is Heideggerian, except that, as Gadamer noted in
1983, he had the vision even before he met Heidegger.[7] Man is
a finite animal who does not have the kind of inscribed answers that instincts represent in animals. Man must rather
think what he is doing.

It is in the context of a speaking civilization that Plato's
Philebos and Aristotle's *Protreptikos* have to be understood, if
they are to be understood at all. Plato's text is a dialogue, and
hence as a piece of "writing," it is as close as it can be to speaking. Similarly, Aristotle's *Protreptikos* is a kind of sermon, and
hence it too is a piece of writing that is much closer to speaking than are Aristotle's other texts. Because both writings are
close to speaking, Gadamer argues, they do not employ terms
whose meanings have been fixed for the sake of attaining scientific knowledge. By this I take Gadamer to mean that "writings" like the Aristotelian *Protreptikos* are designed by their
authors to make their listeners reason. A *protreptikos*—and
I mean the term in a generic sense—has to be interpreted.
There is no other way to make it meaningful. This shift in the

locus of meaning thus throws the burden of intention on the hearer. If a *protreptikos*, any *protreptikos*, means anything at all, its final meaning will be an understanding arrived at as a consequence of the dialectical interplay of speaker and hearer.

By raising the issue of language in his first writing, Gadamer inadvertently raises a question about the locus of meaning. He does this in the 1920s, precisely the same period in which Mikhail Bakhtin was raising the same kind of question about Dostoyevski's poetics, and Gadamer's claims are very similar to those of Bakhtin. Dostoyevski's characters, claims Bakhtin, are indeterminate and hence independent of their author. They work out their characters in Dostoyevski's novels, and hence they determine the *meaning* of the novels at least as much as the author does. Now Gadamer is doing something similar with Plato's dialogues and with Aristotle's *Protreptikos*. He is saying that they do not have fixed answers, determined by the author. They rather raise questions, and hence they provoke the hearer (or the reader) to answer the question for himself or herself, and this reader response is what brings the situation—better, the *situatedness* of the novel—into play. Meaning, in any case, is not author determined. It is rather determined by the reader, and since every reader is differently situated, emphasis is finally on the dialogue between reader and text.

In effect, Gadamer is arguing against the tendency of German *Altertumswissenschaft* to accumulate a body of facts and call that "Greece." He is enlivening the project by reminding us that the authors of classical texts were real human beings with real social problems. Every author no doubt to some extent determines a text to have a fixed meaning, but that meaning reflects the historical circumstances in which the author constructed the text. Since these circumstances change, then so too must meaning change, and indeed change should reflect changing historical circumstances. Every reader, or listener, is thus a kind of author (or authority), reflecting his or her own particular circumstances and hence reconstructing meaning to fit those circumstances. Of course there is a degree of relativism here, but it is usually much less than is made out.

The conventional response to this historicization of meaning is to deny that the original author was subject to historical circumstances. This amounts to a privileging of the original author, and of course it cannot be done for every author. Thus there is unlikely to be much dispute over the character of the meaning intended by Mark Twain or by Friedrich Nietzsche, for they were admittedly influenced by their historical circumstances. They claim to be witnesses to the follies of their times. But insofar as the author or authors claim access to an ahistorical truth—and by this I mean a truth that will not change with time—a real contest will ensue. The Bible is subject to precisely this kind of contest insofar as it is claimed that God is the original author. Reader-response critics will make every effort to demonstrate that each page of the Bible is characterized by errors, inconsistencies, and other indications of its historical rather than divine origins.[8] This is a necessary argument if the locus of authority is to shift from the author to the reader of the Bible. Opponents may admit these inconsistencies, but they will insist there is still a divine truth to be found in the Bible, prior to any and all readings of the text. This divine truth will not change with time.

The Platonic writings are surrounded by this type of controversy. Insofar as the ideas which Plato speaks of are said to be objective, they are necessarily ahistorical, and even though Plato the person was in history, his writings have to be treated as expressions of something else. Plato is accorded roughly the same treatment as a traditionalist Christian would accord to Matthew, Mark, Luke, or John. It is only the rare critic who will claim that Plato, sometimes at least, has no privileged doctrine of ideas. It is much more likely that a well-trained modern reader, coming across a text by Plato that obviously has no doctrine of ideas, will claim either that the text is not by Plato or that it is by an immature Plato or an aged or decrepit Plato. The *Parmenides*, indeed was treated in precisely this fashion in the established German academic world. Every

philological indicator said that the text was by Plato, but because it did not have a doctrine of ideas at its center, Platonic
authorship was denied by no less a classical philologist than
Otto Apelt.[9]

Insofar as the claim is made that Plato has no doctrine of
ideas, then the claimant is compelled to redeem what he has
staked out by demonstrating that Plato's language is irreducibly incomplete, that it is not articulating an answer but is
rather raising a question. One way to do this is to argue that
the language being used is that of a *speaking* culture, for a
speaking language is speaking to someone other than the author and, as such, it invites the response that will complete the
thought. Gadamer, writing in 1927, was not in fact making an
explicit claim about the absence of a doctrine of ideas. But he
was making one of the possible arguments to support such a
claim, and this being the case, we are on fair grounds in concluding that Gadamer was making his first move in the direction of establishing an undoctrinaire Plato.

There was obvious political significance to the kind of implicit claim Gadamer was staking out in his first piece. In the
Germany of the 1920s, Jaeger could be read as supporting the
established authorities, that is to say, state functionaries, professors, and the classical authors of texts. There were no sur-
prises in this position. Gadamer, in contrast, was supporting
the authority of nonestablished "authorities," namely, readers, listeners, and by implication students and lay persons.
Jaeger was much closer to the position carved out by *Altertumswissenschaftler* in the nineteenth century, Gadamer
much closer to the position of the first generation of amateur
philologists, readers like Hölderlin and Humboldt. Gadamer's
Greece was a speaking culture because it was designed to
raise questions, not provide answers. Put differently, Greece
was classical because it had no answers. Its questions rather
than its answers are its enduring classical elements. All of
this indicated that Gadamer was at the very outset of his academic career part of a move away from the state-oriented liberalism of Germany's nineteenth century and toward the more

western, individualistic liberalism that Germany would only fully subscribe to after 1945.

III

It seems unreasonable to expect that Gadamer would introduce one of the main themes of *Truth and Method* as early as his first writing. But this is precisely what he did, and although his comments are brief and specifically directed to the immediate task of correcting Jaeger's conception of Platonic philosophy, all the key points of Gadamer's later argument are touched upon. That is to say, Gadamer introduces the theme of *method*, ascribes to it a fetish for exactness[10] characteristic of the modern desire to attain certain truth, and then goes on to argue that the truth Plato sought was to be attained by *mixture* (of speaker and listener) rather than by measured application of exact ideas.[11] Gadamer's point is to establish that there is truth of sorts outside the certain methods of the sciences, and this of course is one of the themes that is at the center of *Truth and Method*.

In his 1927 paper, Gadamer began his argument by claiming that it was awkward at best to seek a doctrine of method (*Methodenlehre*) in any protreptic writing, but that this was precisely what Jaeger wanted to do. Jaeger held, Gadamer claimed, that in the *Protreptikos* of Aristotle, a certain validity was still accorded to the old Platonic ideal of a mathematically exact method. By method, Gadamer meant a procedure originating in the presupposition that the Ideas could be applied exactly, without interpretation, to worldly reality. Jaeger was doing this in order to set a beginning point for his own developmental history. He would then go on to show how Aristotle drew away from this methodologically oriented Plato to become the flexible thinker of the *Nicomachean Ethics*.

Gadamer of course disagreed. In opposition, he argued that the Plato of the *Philebos*, which as a late Platonic text is roughly contemporary with Aristotle's *Protreptikos*, was itself already drawing away from the classically formulated doctrine of ideas of the *Phaidon*. But Plato did so not by abandoning the ideal of a methodical reconstruction of the realm of Becoming in terms of the realm of Being but rather in terms of a different concept which, as already noted, Gadamer calls *mixing*. "In this manner," Gadamer notes, "the later Plato sought to reconcile the motif of exactness (which was given with the primacy accorded to Being in the ideas) with the actual impurity of human reality."[12]

Aside from the obvious mixing of the thinking of the speaker and the listener, what further meaning does the concept of *mixing* have, and what is its philosophical justification? "The aim of the entire [Platonic] effort," Gadamer argued, "is to limit the claim of *phronesis* [on the one hand] and *hedone* [on the other hand] on the well-being of actual human existence."[13] If we extrapolate this reasoning, then Gadamer's justification of mixing is simple: It records the recognition that man is not simply a thinking being (*phronesis*) but is also a pleasure-seeking animal (*hedone*). In other words, man has a touch of the divine, but only a touch. Plato, supposedly an idealist, turns out to be very much a realist if one pays attention to the theme of hedonism that runs through Plato's writings.

Gadamer was well placed to make just such a recognition insofar as his 1922 doctoral dissertation had traced the theme of desire through Plato's writings.[14] The 1922 dissertation was a standard exercise in which one theme—*Lust*, or desire—was selected and traced through the entirely of Plato's writings. This was a typical and well-established model for doing doctoral dissertations, and in choosing to follow it, the youthful Gadamer was staying to a safe course for gaining a doctorate. When asked in 1986 what his opinion of his doctorate was, Gadamer reflected briefly and then told the following story. He had asked his present wife to read it and give her opinion, and she had told him that if he submitted such a dissertation today, it would have a difficult time getting accepted. It is hard to quarrel with this judgment.

Gadamer drew no daring conclusions from his 1922 doctoral dissertation, but by 1927 he was obviously ready to harvest a major conclusion about Plato. The constant preoccupation with *Lust* demonstrated that Plato was a realist as well as an idealist, and a problem of Plato scholarship was how to reconcile these two seemingly conflicting threads. Put differently, because Plato was both idealist and realist, it was inappropriately one-sided for a Plato scholar to attempt to see Plato as applying the Ideas in an exact mathematical sense to the human condition. It would be more appropriate to mix what is ideal with what is natural and real. Gadamer puts this thought in these words: "Only in a mixture need one seek the Good in this life."[15] By emphasizing *mixture*, Gadamer had already in 1927 committed himself to a *dialectical* approach to Plato. *Mixture* is a synthesis that can be reduced to thesis and antithesis, and Plato, conceived this way, is a thinker whose ethical conclusions can be reduced to a tense relation to the divine longing for exact standards and the worldly desire for bodily pleasure.

Jaeger, needless to say, was not a dialectical thinker. He caricatured Plato by conceiving him as an idealist and thereby determined that his subsequent thinking about Aristotle would be equally undialectical, or one-sided. If Plato was an Idealist, then Aristotle must be a Realist, etc., etc. This kind of thinking is attractive because it simplifies everything and lays it out on a single plane. The mind then need only remember the fundamental principles and follow up by extrapolating their consequences. From such a monological point of view, any dialogical approach looks needlessly complicated, even contradictory. Gadamer's approach to Plato is thus fundamentally different from Jaeger's, and it follows with some consistency that if Jaeger's caricature of Plato is mistaken, so too is his caricature of Aristotle. That is to say, if Gadamer's Plato is a dialogical thinker, then it should not be surprising that Gadamer's Aristotle will also be this.

From this kind of reasoning about the *Philebos*, Gadamer can then move on to another conclusion, this time about the character of the *language* in Aristotle's *Protreptikos*. If Jaeger were to succeed in proving that Aristotle had adopted the Platonic theory of ideas in the *Protreptikos*, then Jaeger would necessarily have to show that Aristotle had adopted a terminological vocabulary. The word to emphasize here is *terminology*, and its meaning is that a word only has a single meaning. Hence a word like *abstinence* remains a mere word as long as it is subject to different interpretations. But as soon as it is given a precise, quantifiable, and hence measurable meaning, then it becomes a term. This is what Gadamer means. It is a point Gadamer had already made in reference to speaking cultures, and now he repeats it in specific reference to Aristotle:

> There is nothing to be said of a unified scientific terminology in these arguments. *We rather see the terminological composition changing from argument to argument* [Gadamer's italics]. And moreover, what is revealed in all these arguments is the effort, so far as it is possible, not to burden [the overall argument] with terminology.[16]

This argument about language correlates with the argument made earlier about thinking. That is to say, monological thinking reveals itself in terminological language. Each word, or term, will have a clear and distinct meaning that is determined by clear and distinct principles. In contrast, a dialogical foundation in thinking will provide circumstantial evidence of itself by means of the absence of a terminological language. Words will have more than one meaning, and often these will be in contradiction with each other, thereby reflecting the dialogical basis of thinking. Furthermore, if a thinker is at all aware of his own dialogical basis, then he can begin a *play* with words. He can, like Plato, engage in irony and say almost anything with tongue in cheek. Or he can, like the early Gadamer, restore the meaning of contradiction to philosophy by recognizing that every claim (*Anspruch*) is necessarily addressed to someone and seeks to elicit a contradiction or counterclaim (*Widerspruch*) as a necessary step on the way to agreement. By claiming that Aristotle did not have a terminological language, Gadamer was in effect claiming that Aristotle was not the kind of thinker Jaeger would like to have him be. He was, in sum, a dialogical thinker.

What then finally is Gadamer to make of the Aristotelian *Protreptikos*? His conclusion is stated very tentatively, yet has all the earmarkings of a significant finding. In a footnote in an early section of this paper, Gadamer suggests that the *Protreptikos* might in fact be dialogue.[17] Now this is a remarkable suggestion considering the conventional wisdom that holds that *all* of Aristotle's dialogues have been lost, but it is nonetheless a suggestion that flows smoothly from Gadamer's reasoning. That is to say, if the classical Greek age was a *speaking* rather than a *writing* age, then it was not given to the creation of a terminological language. Since Aristotle was not creating a terminological language in the *Protreptikos*, it follows—at least it is suggested—that Aristotle's *Protreptikos* was a piece of written speech. For Gadamer this means that it incorporated dialogue, and in his footnote he attempts to tease out the dialogue, or at least to suggest that it can be heard out. What he then "hears" is Aristotle making an effort to review the opinions of other thinkers, and this suggests to him that what he is reading is not a monologue but rather a smoothed-over dialogue with other thinkers. In sum, what Gadamer is doing here is demonstrating as best he can that *writing* originates in *speaking*, better: that language has a certain order of development, and it is the opposite of what Jaeger presupposes.

Since Gadamer had already made this same point in a different way in the same paper, it is worth thematizing as the central conclusion of this 1927 publication. Language is not initially *writing* which is then laboriously deconstructed into *speaking*. If this were the case, then we would have to admit that rationality was an iron cage from which we were always trying to escape. In a scientific and bureaucratized civilization, such as the Central European of Gadamer's youth, it often did seem that *writing precedes speaking*, but for Gadamer this is not the primordial truth. If it were, then truth could only be attained by method, and any falling short of methodical exactness into speaking could only be justified as a pleasant interlude, a playful relaxing, before getting back to the serious business of leading an exact life. But this is not Gadamer's point.

The really interesting argument of this small quarrel with Werner Jaeger over the primordial structure of the discipline of philology is that *speaking precedes writing*, indeed, that writing is either a shorthand way of speaking or it is a fallen form of speaking. When writing is the former, then we can tease out of it an original dialectical structure, as Gadamer suggestively did with the Aristotelian *Protreptikos*. When writing is the latter, when it is a fallen form of speech, then at least in the field of ethics it threatens to become a form of moralizing. Gadamer does not argue this in his first piece, but he will later on, and hence it is not entirely inappropriate to anticipate it here.

Why should this particular order be the case? Why, that is, should *speaking precede writing*? If I understand the Gadamer of 1927 correctly, the answer is not mysterious or profound. Speaking and writing are metaphors or synonyms for basic attitudes we take up toward life. A speaking culture privileges the quest, and it does so because the quest retains a primordial awareness of the coming and going of Being, or rather its indeterminate character. Transferred to the formality of philosophy, the privileging of the quest takes shape as a privileging of the question. The magic of the question for philosophy, its *thaumatic* quality, lies precisely in its indeterminacy. Then second, if we transfer this attitude to the social plane, what we recognize is that the characterization "speaking culture" is a synonym for the culture of Weimar Germany for the simple but compelling reason that values were everywhere in question in Weimar Germany. It was a culture in crisis, which is to say that it did not have answers but did have a critical attitude toward the answers of the German past.

It would not be at all surprising if a young philologist in Weimar Germany made a simple transfer of the basic attitude we are describing and applied it to classical Greece. Classical Greece was a culture in crisis, according to Gadamer, which is to say that it was a culture torn between speaking and writing. It was still a speaking culture, but it was threatened with becoming a writing culture. It was threatened, that is, with a loss of understanding of its own values, above all the value of the endless conversation that is at the base of any real speaking culture. This was the sickness, with dialectical philosophy the proffered cure.

With this kind of conclusion we are finally in a good position to turn to Gadamer's habilitation thesis. Its title is curious and is perhaps misleading. Easy to translate, it is best rendered into English as *Plato's Dialectical Ethics*.[18] Yet when we read the first paragraph of Gadamer's Preface, we are taken aback. He claims that his intent is not to show that Plato's ethics are dialectical but rather that Plato's dialectics themselves are ethical.

IV

Plato dialektische Ethik begins by taking up the argument left off at the end of the 1927 Jaeger piece. In fact, Jaeger is mentioned in the first paragraph of the Introduction, where Gadamer notes that it was Jaeger's interpretation of Aristotle that made a reconsideration of Plato's *Philebos* imperative.[19] I would like to argue, however, that the real beginning of Gadamer's habilitation thesis and of his early conception of philosophical hermeneutics is to be found a few pages later, buried in a footnote, and furthermore a footnote that was altered in the 1983 edition of Gadamer's collected works. The 1983 footnote reads:

The method consciousness of this restriction determines throughout the scientific claim of the *Nicomachean Ethics*. An interpretation of the *Nicomachean
Ethics* in respect to the problem of its scientific character is sorely called for. [In pursuit of this problem I
eventually drew philosophical consequences which led
to my work with hermeneutics. (*Truth and Method* and
the continuation of the philosophical hermeneutic in respect to this "practical philosophy" are to be found in
volumes one and two of the *Collected Works*)].[20]

The words in square brackets were added in 1983, or therea-
bouts. They suggest, correctly in my opinion, that Gadamer's
life work began with the 1928 reflections on *method consciousness* to which Gadamer was referring in the footnote. What
the 1983 footnote does not tell, however, is that Gadamer was
fully aware of the significance of this beginning fifty years earlier, in 1928/31, when he wrote the original footnote. In fact,
the 1983 footnote slightly changes the wording of the original
1928/31 footnote and thereby makes the 1983 bracketed comment look like an afterthought. The words ". . . is sorely
needed" [*täte Not*] do not appear in the 1931 edition.
In their place are the words ". . . the author hopes to present
at a later time" [*hofft der Verf. später vorzulegen*].[21] Now
Gadamer did not mean later in the book he was then writing.
He would not have used the word "hope" but rather would simply have referred to the later pages. Gadamer means later in
his career. What Gadamer was doing was simply thinking
aloud. He was planning his agenda and laying out what he
would do once he had gotten through this academic requirement of producing and publishing a habilitation thesis.

All of this becomes something more than a mere coincidence
if we refer back to the text and ask what Gadamer was talking
about when he introduced the term *method consciousness* in
1927. He does so at the point of making a set of remarks about
the nature of concepts and conceptualization and how Aris-

totle, in moving toward a mode of philosophizing dependent upon concepts, had drawn a curtain between himself and Plato which made, or would make, the Aristotelian interpretation of the Platonic doctrine of ideas so problematic.

The argument that follows runs thus: Gadamer's claim is that Aristotle was the creator of a philosophical science of ethics for the compellingly simple reason that he had indeed moved away from Idealism and toward Realism. That is to say, the Aristotle of the *Nicomachean Ethics* privileged a putative Reality in a way that Plato, ever the dialectician, never did, and hence Aristotle determined himself to a different mode of analysis. In specific reference to ethics, Gadamer puts this thought as follows: Plato's determinations about ethics are *privative*, meaning that they are deduced from thinking about the Idea of the Good. Aristotle's in contrast are *positive*, meaning that they are drawn from a logic immanent to real human relations.[22]

The key to understanding Aristotle's method consciousness lies in Gadamer's term 'restriction' (*Einschränkung*), for what Gadamer claims is that a Realist ethics is compelled to draw the logic of its concepts from the actual way human beings relate in the world, and this can result in nothing more than "a certain assistance" (*eine gewisse Hilfe*) to living life.[23] This is a restriction of what Plato had intended. Positivism, for this is what Aristotle is introducing, is committed to a preexisting realm of factual relations. Precisely because this world is presupposed to be real—that is to say, composed of established facts which would exist whether or not we observed them—it can be conceptualized, the concepts can be systematically organized, and the real world can be assisted, perhaps even reordered, according to these concepts. The consciousness that presupposes this real world is a method consciousness.

I have hesitated to introduce the terms *Idealism* and *Realism* for the simple reason that they can easily be taken in the crude sense and thus serve to derail Gadamer's main line of argument. The terms serve to create a gulf between Plato and Aristotle which is impossible to bridge and thus go against

Gadamer's main intent. It is best to construe Gadamer to be making a mild rather than a strong claim about Aristotle's Realism. I believe this position is borne out by Gadamer's use of the term *restriction*. Plato and Aristotle are not really opposed to each other as Idealist and Realist. It is rather that Aristotle has lapsed into a one-sided position, one that represents a "restriction" on the whole of ethical possibilities.

I thus think that Gadamer's treatment of Aristotle at the outset of his habilitation thesis represents a refinement of his earlier basic distinction between a *speaking* and a *writing* culture. Reality, whatever it is—a painting by Rembrandt, a play by Shakespeare, or even a dialogue by Plato—is presupposed to be unambiguous. It thereby lends itself to the construction of a terminological language, or rather a language that is unambiguous in its meaning because it can be referred back to that certain Reality. Such a terminological language lends itself to writing, because writing has a definitive and final quality to it. Or if it is spoken, a terminological language tends toward the monologue of a lecture: There is no need to have dialogue because the meanings of things are fixed.

But then how can we be certain that Gadamer is making only a mild claim about Aristotle and is rejecting the strong claim about the Realist/Idealist break between Plato and Aristotle? Quite simply because Gadamer says as much. He does not even bother to reject the crude arguments to the effect that Aristotle was a scoundrel setting up a strawman or that Aristotle was so stupid as to have misunderstood Plato. Gadamer's claim is that Aristotle did not misunderstand Plato at all: "That Aristotle misunderstood Plato is a piece of information rightly taken to be an impossibility . . ." Gadamer says in his habilitation thesis.[24] Why, then, is Aristotle so wrong about Plato? Gadamer's answer is that the riddle is a symptomatic expression of the problem of philosophy itself. Plato's language possesses a three-dimensional reality, and Aristotle the realist, committed as he is to conceptualizing the real world, is compelled to treat philosophy itself the same way. This makes Aristotle into the founder of scientific, academic philosophy, and Plato into what might be called a *pre-Aristotelian* or, better still, a proto-philosopher. It is a position Gadamer would like to get his Plato into.

A conceptualization of Plato, Gadamer goes on to argue in his habilitation thesis, can produce nothing more than a *flattening* of Plato, such as is attained when real life is photographed, put on slides and then represented by being *projected* onto a wall.[25] By this means, Aristotle achieves an unambivalent and reproduceable philosophical text—this is the condition for the emergence of a scientific, academic philosophy—but the price Aristotle pays for this achievement is high. It is to be calculated in terms of a lost Platonic multidimensionality. Whether Aristotle is aware that his method consciousness is perhaps playing a trick on him is a question not considered by Gadamer. His claim is rather that the Plato Aristotle criticizes is a conceptualized Plato, and this is already not the Plato of the dialogues.

If I read Gadamer correctly at this key point, he is suggesting that the origins of Aristotle's Realism lie in the character of *language*. Aristotle had discovered that language need not be used in a three-dimensional poetic fashion. Language could rather be flattened out and used for analytical purposes. A flattened-out language would take an undismembered reality and lay it out in sequential fashion, with each word standing for a concept and each concept standing for a facet or piece of the reality. What Aristotle forgot was that a conceptualized reality and reality itself were not the same thing. Ironically, Plato, with his three-dimensional language, was always closer to putative reality than the analytical Aristotle, but Plato was only this by remaining with a poetic language of action. This much Aristotle failed to grasp: When he turned his analytical talents on Plato, all he could do was flatten out Plato and describe him as a one-sided Idealist.

I can perhaps best get across what Gadamer means by taking an example from elsewhere. A work of art of any kind, whether it be a painting, a play by Shakespeare, or a dialogue

by Plato, presents itself to the mind as a three-dimensional reality. It speaks, as it were, the language of action, and we read
this language not only by looking at it but also by hearing it
and if need be by feeling the words in our mouths. This is why
we tell our students to read poems aloud and to press home
certain words. We are only saying that poems are works of art
and are to be taken as sensual wholes, for it is only at that
level that we gain the immediacy of the experience they are
conveying.

But then along comes the art historian, and what he or she
offers is a secondhand, conceptualized version of the work of
art. The emphasis is now on seeing and seeing alone, and the
language is different. We read books and see slides, and if we
hear lectures, then we are not hearing the work of art but are
rather hearing *about* the work of art. We are being told how
we should see. We are hearing about the flattened and sequentially arranged work of art. We are hearing a lecture, not the
work of art. We leave the lecture with the illusion that we
know the work, perhaps without ever having experienced it
firsthand.

This distinction between art and the art historian is not far
removed from what Gadamer is trying to say of the relationship between Plato and Aristotle. Gadamer does not argue
that Aristotle was mistaken in his concept of Plato. He rather
argues that "all scientific philosophy is Aristotelianism, insofar as it is the labor of the concept. . . ."[26] Moreover, Gadamer
continues, Platonic philosophy can only be philosophically interpreted by taking up the method consciousness of Aristotle.
The immediate experience that Plato's dialogues have more to
them than Aristotelian method consciousness conveys is an
experience which, because of its immediacy, does not let itself
be communicated. Thus Gadamer:

> It stands on the margin of all Plato interpretation, just
> as experience stands on the margin of all conceptual
> analysis [*Begriffsarbeit*], namely the insight that all at-

tempts to signify succeed only by making things unambivalent and one-dimensional, and insofar as this activity opens things up, it also distorts things.[27]

One is then compelled to ask how Gadamer is going to proceed to come to terms with Plato's thinking if analysis, the
treating of Plato's thinking in terms of concepts, is so inescapable. Surprisingly, Gadamer admits that he necessarily must
follow the same path:

> Just as all reflection on the relationship of the living to
> the concept can itself only be conceived in terms of the
> concept, similarly the Platonic existence of philosophy
> can only be conceived insofar as the scholar himself re-
> peats a projection into the conceptual such as Aristotle
> undertook.[28]

That Gadamer means what he says, at least for the long first
chapter of his habilitation thesis, is indicated several pages
later when he introduces the concept of *play*, only to immediately disavow it:

> . . . insofar as it [Gadamer's interpretation] takes seri-
> ously that about which Plato is here speaking, it also
> takes what he is saying more seriously than Plato in-
> tended it to be taken. The ironic suspense, not only at
> those points where everyone senses the irony but also
> throughout, that determines the character of the Pla-
> tonic writings, will be omitted completely from . . . [this
> interpretation]. . . . It adopts the attitude of a humor-
> less listener to one of those conversations thought to
> be worthwhile only for the sake of the report one can
> make of it, [and Gadamer does this] because he seeks to
> make clear the means by which Plato plays his serious
> game.[29]

This adequately describes how Gadamer will treat Plato in
the first chapter of his habilitation thesis, but it does not ade-

quately convey how he will transcend Aristotle's humorless method consciousness to attain a truth about Plato that no analysis of Plato can convey. This is the truth of what Gadamer called the immediate experience of Plato, and by this I take Gadamer to mean the unmediated, multidimensional experience of the Platonic writings.

V

Plato does not have a doctrine of ethics (or ethical ideas), Gadamer claims, and this makes him into a Socratic (for Socrates had no doctrines of any type) and the undoctrinaire Socrates into Plato's *Gestalt*.[30] Plato's task was to take the unliterary but obviously exemplary existence of Socrates and give it literary expression. Hence, if I may draw the conclusion clearly suggested by Gadamer's claims, the Platonic dialogues are nothing less than a series of *Gestalt*-biographies of the figure called the "Platonic Socrates." More significantly, Plato is not really a philosopher at all for Gadamer, at least in the conventional sense of the term. He is rather a literary creator, and his creations will be found in the shape his language takes. When Gadamer finally addresses the three-dimensional existence of the Platonic Socrates, he reverts fully to the ideals of the Stefan George Circle.

What follows from this? That is to say, how does one go about writing a book called *Platos dialektische Ethik* if one conceives Plato as a *Gestalt*-biographer? The first thing to note is perhaps obvious: The analysis will not be of Plato alone but rather of the figure of Socrates that is being formed. Well and good, but this raises a specific problem of classical scholarship. One must be clear about which Socrates one is concerned. Obviously, as Gadamer noted in his 1983 letter to Richard Bernstein, his interest was in the figure of the *Platonic Socrates*, but what this entailed needs to be established.[31]

First of all, a distinction must be made between the *histori-cal Socrates* and the *literary Socrates*, a basic distinction on which every classical philologist would agree.[32] The histori-cal Socrates is made up of what few undisputed facts we have on Socrates. We know that he lived, philosophized, and was tried and executed for his activities. Perhaps these facts can be elaborated a little, but not much. The point is that we know very little that is certain about the historical Socrates. *Alter-tumswissenschaft*, or more generally positivism, thus fails when it comes to the challenge of constructing an adequate Socrates. We are of necessity forced back onto a literary fabri-cation of Socrates.

The literary Socrates is derived from three sources: Xeno-phon, Aristophanes, and Plato. The *Xenophonic Socrates* is a rather routine character who could not conceivably have been much of an inspiration to anyone, except perhaps the later Stoics. Not surprisingly like his creator Xenophon, the Xeno-phonic Socrates was a teacher of young men who held forth in polished speeches but was never very profound. The *Aristo-phanic Socrates*, in contrast, is a much more lively character but is hardly admirable and is best recalled as something of a fool. He gives ridiculous speeches from ridiculous positions and is anything but profound. He would be as much consigned to oblivion in the modern world as the Socrates of Xenophon is if it were not for Nietzsche, who fully and vindictively resur-rected Aristophanes' Socrates.

So finally we come to the third literary version of Socrates, and this is the *Platonic Socrates*. This figure is familiar and perhaps hackneyed. He is profoundly philosophical, sharply questioning, and obviously a moral paradigm. But my point is not to suggest that the Platonic Socrates is an unambiguous figure. On the contrary, because Plato is the deeply ironic writer he is, choices must still be made about what the Pla-tonic Socrates is. Plato, that is, distinguishes himself from Xenophon and Aristophanes by virtue of the fact that his Soc-rates is not such a clear-cut case. Is, for example, the Platonic Socrates really so ignorant as he makes himself out to be, or is not the otherwise despised Thrasymachus correct when he tells Socrates to come off it in the first book of the *Republic*? Would that the answer were clear from Plato's text, but it is not. We like to pretend that Plato thought only pleasant thoughts about his Socrates, but this too is not so clear. And also, why is it that Socrates plays such a commanding role in the early dialogues but then gradually disappears? Was Plato getting old, or was he losing interest, or had Socrates served his purpose and been laid to rest, in much the same manner that Conan Doyle laid Sherlock Holmes to rest? We have no clear answers to these questions.

The point here is fundamental to the understanding of hermeneutics. In the case of the Platonic Socrates, there is no way we can locate meaning in the intention of the author. The Platonic Socrates is irreducibly ambivalent. Hence, the focus on the creation of meaning shifts fully to the reader. Could Plato have intended this shift in the responsibility for creating meaning? We shall never know. But we can be certain that at least in this one case, there is no escaping the conclusion that the construction of the Platonic Socrates is reader-determined. Hence, the chief value of the Platonic Socrates is that, when constructed by an interpreter, the construction then serves as a standard of immanent criticism not of Plato but of the interpreter.

Therefore, the way Gadamer constructs the Platonic Socrates will tell us a lot more about Gadamer than it will about Plato. It will only tell us about Plato if Gadamer writes a distinctly academic book and airs all sides of the conventional questions. But Gadamer has already told us in so many words that Plato wrote a *Gestalt*-biography of Socrates, and this signals Gadamer's belief that Plato made choices and settled for a certain kind of Socrates, specifically, a heroic figure. It is hard to believe that the twenty-seven-year-old Gadamer, well versed as he then was in Plato scholarship, did not realize that it was his own choice that he was describing. He had no intention of writing yet one more academic rehash of the Platonic Socrates. His intent was to write his own *Gestalt*-biography.

Hence we are now looking at the early Gadamer in the mirror of the choices he made about his Platonic Socrates. The first choice Gadamer made was perhaps the most controversial of his book. He claimed that the existence-ideal of the Platonic Socrates was not at all that of a philosopher who stood aside from political questions. The existence-ideal of Socrates was fully political, and hence the writings of Plato must be understood finally in political terms.[33] The significance of this choice was sketched out earlier: It sets Plato outside the framework of analytic, academic philosophy. It is a choice which squares with Gadamer's earlier choice to accept the significance of Plato's three-dimensional language.

To back up this extraordinary claim, the young Gadamer made a move that had to be taken as provocative in 1927. Yet it was a move that had to be made if he were to support his claim about the Platonic Socrates being basically political. Gadamer fully accepted the authenticity of the *Seventh Letter* of Plato.[34] There is no point in going over the trivial philological arguments for and against the authenticity of this famous letter because they alone can never decide the question of authenticity. The problem is philosophical rather than philological. And the philosophical problem in the *Seventh Letter* is that Plato says that he turned to philosophy for political reasons. Therefore, if we are to believe the *Seventh Letter*, Plato was not really a philosopher. Plato was rather a politician, although perhaps it would be easier on twentieth-century ears to say that he was a would-be *Founder* of states. Philosophy was therefore the continuation of politics by other means. Now regardless of the philological arguments, such a claim is on its face extraordinarily challenging to the vision of Plato as the purest of philosophers.

Yet the authenticity of the *Seventh Letter* can also be argued on purely philosophical grounds: If Plato had no doctrine of ideas, if his ideas were merely starting points for conversation, if he had no doctrine of ethics, if he was intent on using language to provoke public debate in a *speaking* culture, if his words did not have determinate meanings, then it followed logically from these several different perspectives that Plato was nothing other than a politician. Once again, the term *politician* may be troublesome, but what is meant by it is simply that Plato fully accepts the *situated* quality of his own thinking. He is not in the least otherworldly, seeking after eternal truths, but is rather out to vindicate the world as it is and as it appears. At first glance, it seems as though Gadamer was taking a risk in accepting the authenticity of the *Seventh Letter*. Upon reflection it becomes clear that there was no risk at all. This was the only thing he could do. To not accept the authenticity of the *Seventh Letter* would have been fully in contradiction with everything Gadamer had already staked out in his first piece on Werner Jaeger.

The second choice that Gadamer made in reference to his Platonic Socrates was to accept the Socratic profession of ignorance, and this acceptance squares fully with the insistence on Plato's political origin.[35] To view the matter in the opposed fashion, if the Platonic Socrates had claimed privileged knowledge, then he would have been no different from most if not all of his interlocutors. What distinguishes him politically and radicalizes him is the claim to have no privileged knowledge. This one move makes Socrates into a revolutionary, and it also distinguishes his kind of politics from the kind practiced in the existing Athenian state.

But let us be clear about what Gadamer's emphatic insistence on the Socratic profession of ignorance adds up to. It is above all an indirect way of claiming that Plato had no doctrine of ideas. That is to say, if Plato did have a doctrine of objective ideas, would not the Platonic Socrates have been a spokesman for those ideas? But the Platonic Socrates, according to Gadamer, only professes ignorance on ethical matters. Is this not a reflection back on his master, and does it not tell us something we already know about Gadamer, namely, that he is party to that minority of academic philologians who dispute the claim of the German academic establishment about Plato having a doctrine of ideas? What is exciting about Gadamer at this point is that he is not simply and flatly claiming that Plato has no doctrine of ideas; he is rather constructing Socrates according to that radical claim. He is also constructing, or revealing, himself as a thinker who is opposed to the notion that certain, fixed, prescribed *knowledge* is at the center of philosophy.

Let us now pass on to a third Gadamerian choice. It is difficult to tell from the text of Gadamer's habilitation thesis what he means by the term *Athenian state*.[36] Narrowly, of course, Gadamer must mean the state that condemned Socrates to death, but it is much more interesting to construct the notion of the Athenian *state* broadly and argue that Gadamer was referring to all those conversational antagonists who claimed they *knew* what the virtues were. In this respect, the failure of the Athenian state was a failure of self-consciousness, much like the failure of self-consciousness of the Central European state of Gadamer's childhood. It, the Athenian state, did not recognize that its knowledge was situated. Put differently, the Athenian political elite, precisely because it claimed to know what the virtues were, was depoliticizing itself and thereby bringing about the cultural crisis of the Greek Enlightenment. The Platonic Socrates, in contrast, was the very model of the statesman when he professed ignorance of the meaning of the virtues. Since they were situated truths, they simply could not be known, except as prejudices characteristic of the Athenian state.

Because Socrates does recognize his situatedness, he qualifies, according to Gadamer, as *the statesman* for Plato. Here then, not in the doctrine of ideas, is to be found the origin of Platonic political philosophy.[37] But the claim that the Platonic Socrates is the real statesman of Athens has another, more local significance. It sets the stage for an important subsequent publication of Gadamer called "Plato's Educational State."[38] The kernel of its idea is here laid out: Plato does not intend to reform the Athenian state but rather intends to start from scratch. This means that Socrates' project is to create new men who will be capable of acting as founders of states. Their souls must be shaped, and this means that they must be educated in philosophy. This entire project will be aimed at achieving an understanding of something we cannot know, being situated beings. This is the *Idea of the Good*, and with this idea, Gadamer introduces the central claim of his first book and, arguably, his life's work.

Gadamer's Platonic Socrates provides the first reliable glimpse we have of Gadamer's own political thinking. He, like many of his contemporaries, despairs of the existing state of things, although he makes no direct criticism of the Weimar state. He thus migrates inwardly to a state that is above all cultivated, and first of all this means that it makes no brash knowledge claims that stand in the way of artistic creation. Gadamer's state is a *Kulturstaat*, and specifically it is a *speaking* culture that stands over against the Central European reality of a *writing* culture. Gadamer's thinking resembles that of Humboldt and Schiller in the 1790s, and equally it resembles the thinking of the Stefan George Circle. I am of course stretching things by applying Gadamer's construction of Socratic Athens to the Weimar of the 1920s, but I think the transfer is justified by the nature of the Platonic Socrates. Gadamer had to make choices, and they were bound to reflect the historical circumstances of his own time and profession. He too was a situated being, and his situation was that of Weimar Germany.

In finishing up his Introduction to *Platos dialektische Ethik*, Gadamer finally adopted a method of interpretation appropriate to his grasp of Platonic philosophy. Negatively stated, Gadamer's 1928 method was not one of holding fast to Plato's conceptual apparatus and building a unified system out of his teachings in order to then return to the individual dialogues and criticize their conclusions and arguments. Rather, the Gadamerian method is to also be *under way*. It is to go along with the rhythm and sequence of the questions and therefore to be a questioner. Only under this presupposition is there anything of a doctrine in Plato. Gadamer goes on to argue once again that a terminologically fixed approach to Plato can yield sharp and impressive results, but they are not true to the thinking they are investigating. Gadamer's Plato interpretation would rather seek within the flexibility of Platonic language to work out the tendencies toward meaning that are in Plato, precisely the results that slip past the conceptual framework that Aristotle applies to Plato.

Gadamer then attempts to locate precisely what is different about his method: A conceptual framework such as Aristotle's will miss that which may be most valuable because it will explain only that which the restricted method is prepared to explain. Other things it will take for granted as *self-evident*, which means that these things will not be explained. The problem with analytical philosophy, then, is that it inadvertently *privileges* the self-evident. Gadamer would privilege nothing. His interpretative method will seek to understand that which claims to be understandable of itself [*was sich von selbst versteht* or *das Selbstverständliche*].[39] That which claims to be understandable was not always so. It represents a difficult and lost way of understanding, one that has become the most primordial form of knowledge. Precisely what we take most for granted has to be questioned most intensely because it stands at the base of our knowledge.

I hesitate to claim that what Gadamer is here identifying is what would later come to be called *prejudices*, yet if by the term *prejudices* we understand forms of knowledge that are privileged in the deepest sense and hence go untested, then that which claims to be understandable of itself is close to a prejudice. There are elements of knowledge of which we are ignorant, which is to say that they are elements of the subconscious, and precisely because of their tendency to operate behind our backs, they have much more determining power over us than any conscious presupposition of our knowledge. They are elements of *factical Dasein* insofar as they determine the conscious categories in terms of which we know whatever we claim to know. It is these unconscious presuppositions that Gadamer's 1928 method was after.

VI

It is now possible to see why and how Gadamer's version of the "Platonic Socrates" is a significant advance on Friedemann's argument of fourteen years earlier.[40] Nietzsche had looked scornfully on Plato because he took him to be a dialectical thinker. There is no question that Nietzsche understood Plato as well as any classical philologist in nineteenth-century Germany, but there is reason to believe that Nietzsche's concept of *dialectics* was colored by Hegel's thinking, specifically by the latter's figure of the master-slave relationship. As Gilles Deleuze has pointed out, Nietzsche rejected dialectics as a mode of thinking because he saw in it a model of the kind of Christian moralizing that he despised.[41] Hegel's paradigmatic master-slave relationship is for Nietzsche one that is determined by the slave's point of view, not the master's. It made sense, according to Deleuze, for the slave to see himself as master, but it made no sense at all for the master to see himself in the mirror image of the slave. This would lead to feelings of pity and the like, and these were not elements of a master morality in Nietzsche's view.

Insofar as Nietzsche saw the "Platonic Socrates" in these terms, then he was bound to scorn him. And insofar as the concept of *dialectics* in Gadamer's habilitation thesis was drawn from Hegel, then Gadamer's "Platonic Socrates" is a reconstruction of the character Nietzsche despised. But close examination of the Gadamerian discourse on language, as it developed in his first article and in the Introduction to the habilitation thesis, reveals that Gadamer's concept of *dialectics* is really more a matter of free and unconstrained *dialogue*. Gadamer writes in a superficial sense of circular relationships in which affirmations call forth negations, as, for example, when he notes that a claim (*Spruch*) calls forth a counterclaim (*Widerspruch*). But these moments are seldom in the early Gadamer. His real argument is quite different.

Gadamer is striving to liberate *speaking* from *writing,* an effort consistent with the intent to construct an overman who will satisfy the Nietzschean requirement of being free. Such a Socrates does not see language as a method for deciphering preexisting, objective ideas. This is Platonism in the worst sense of the term, and such Platonism is not politics. Gadamer's "Platonic Socrates" is committed to dialogue as well as to politics, and this much enables us to arrive at a very preliminary sketch of Gadamer's concept of *politics* at the outset of this study of his early thinking. Politics is not a prescribed activity in which language is used as a method to get at the objective truth. Politics is rather a completely unconstrained activity, appropriate for an overman, and conducted in a spoken language that heroically professes ignorance of any prescribed truth. Also, the recurrent concept of dialogue, if it means anything at all, means that politics is not an activity keyed to individual heroism. It is an activity that demands a multiplicity of overmen, each willing to admit ignorance of a prescribed truth, each willing to discourse until agreement is reached. However much I would like to call this political thinking the makings of a radical democratic theory, it is more a matter of radical aristocratic theory. It is in any case not a radical monarchical theory, and hence the conclusion that the philosopher must be king or the king a philosopher is inappropriate. It is more a matter of philosophers becoming overmen, or overmen philosophers.

4

The Gestalt
of
Platonic Argument

I

After his Introduction, Gadamer begins *Platos dialektische Ethik* with a first chapter made up of eight sections and running, in Volume 5 of the *Gesammelte Werke*, approximately sixty pages.[1] This first chapter is entitled "On Platonic Dialectics" and contains an intensely developed theoretical framework. It describes, I believe, not simply the best thinking that the young Gadamer could muster at this stage of his budding career but also a full-blown philosophical hermeneutics and hence a foundation that would serve Gadamer for the rest of his long career as an academic philosopher. Each of the eight sections can be separately treated but finally all hang together and gain additional meaning from each other. In this chapter, I shall treat each section separately and then conclude by pulling together the common strands into an single overview of Gadamer's early thinking.

Gadamer begins with a reference to Werner Jaeger's developmental model but quickly sidesteps its positivistic characteristics to ask a more philosophical question. The problem is not *that* Aristotle developed out of Plato and Plato in turn out of Socrates but *why*.[2] That is to say, the question, more sharply put, is why Aristotle's apodictic, which does not require the agreement of a conversation partner, develops out of Plato's dialectic, which so manifestly proceeds on the basis of conversational agreement.

Put slightly differently, the problem is as follows: Socrates engaged in *dialogue*, and this was a matter of conversation with an Other whose agreement was in fact always needed to keep the conversation going. Plato engaged in *dialectic*, which is manifestly in agreement with Socratic dialogue as a type of proceeding, only more refined. It too required the agreement of an Other, only the Other was now internalized. Aristotle, however, engaged in what is here called *apodictic*, which means that Aristotle spoke from a foundation of certainty and therefore did not require the agreement of a conversation partner. How can this be, which is to say, how can something that does not require agreement develop out of something that requires agreement?

The problem can be put yet another way to assure that it has a distinctly contemporary edge. Aristotle appears to be something of a foundationalist, by which I mean that he presupposes the existence of an agreed-upon Reality which serves as a reference for his statements and gives them the certainty that allows Aristotle to pass lightly over the need for conversational agreement. Plato, whose thinking is the main thread of this introduction, does not work this way. He, like Socrates, presupposes the need for agreement originating in the speech of another. Therefore Plato proposes no foundation other than that of a shared willingness to reach agreement about fundamentals. How can Aristotle, the Realist, be the product of the thinking of Plato, the dialectician?

In answering his own question, Gadamer reverts to one of the most basic themes of Heideggerian thinking, namely that

of the *situatedness* of human beings. Indeed, in this first section, Gadamer claims that his interpretation is phenomen-
ological and defines phenomenology as a retracing of human
knowledge back to its primordial (*ursprünglich*) source in human existence.[3] More specifically, factical human existence is
the source of all sensory knowledge and, hence, the beginning
of all philosophical reflection. In respect to Plato, this phenom-
enological reduction provides an explanation of what dialectic
is.

Classical Greek dialectics, according to Gadamer, originated in the Eleatic philosophers' critique of sensory knowledge. In the *Gorgias* this kind of negative dialectic is a matter
of putting forth what speaks for and what speaks against a
thing. Initially it looks like mere play, a back-and-forth game
which leads nowhere in particular. But in the *Parmenides*
Plato claimed that this was a very serious wordsgame, and in
the *Sophist*, he went on to reveal that dialectic had a positive
side which justified it. In spite of the fact that one thing is de-
monstrably different things to different people, Gadamer argues, language (*logos*) continues to address it as one thing.
This demonstrates, according to Gadamer, the fact of reconcil-
iation (*Verständigung*) through reason (also *logos*).[4] Things,
whatever else they are, are determined by reason. They re-
ceive their unifying certainty through a dialectical process of
thinking in which antithetical positions are synthesized.

It might help to put this more simply: There are no objective
ideas behind things, recognizable as essences when we look at
a thing. Therefore when I utter the word "tree" while pointing at certain things made of wood with leaves on them, I am
not uttering a word which is identical with the essence of the
thing I am pointing at. There are in "reality" (if I may use this
term) many things, but reason sorts through the many to find
the one agreed-upon common strand that gives us our idea of
the thing. Ideas are thus coeval with language, and hence conversation aimed at reaching agreement about what words
mean is an adequate way of representing what happens in the
mind's effort to come to terms, so to speak, with the flux of re-

ality. Once again we see that Plato does not have a doctrine of ideas expressed in his language, according to Gadamer. It is rather the other way round: He has language (*logos*) which works to constitute ideas of reality.

To translate this line of thought into the terminology of contemporary philosophy, Gadamer is arguing that *theory precedes facts*. There are no facts unless we are first given a theoretical framework in which to recognize a fact, and this theoretical framework is constructed dialectically through language. Theorizing, if I understand Gadamer correctly, is the beginning of knowledge.[5] What we have prior to theorizing is a kind of naive Realism (commonsense realism) which fails to recognize how theoretical we always already are. Therefore naive Realism takes facts for granted. The initial destruction of this naive Realism in Eleatic criticism led to a sustained effort to use language to construct more adequate theories, and it is Plato's achievement to have discovered the positive possibilities of this new use of language.

II

In the second section of his introductory chapter, called "Conversation and *Logos*," Gadamer continues the line of argumentation initiated in the first section. There he had gone on from a consideration of Plato to argue that science is a movement away from the flux of sensory knowledge toward *techne* and finally *theoria*. He argued that both *techne* and *theoria* were able to stabilize sensory impressions and find something permanent which could be communicated. Now in this second section Gadamer begins to make his case for conversation by claiming that *original speech* is a common having to do with something.[6] The argument parallels the earlier argument on *techne* and *theoria*, but it is still worthwhile repeating in its essentials. The only thing I want to insist on at this point is that the term *original* not be thought of in a diachronic sense as indicating a point distant in past time. A better term, one more in accord with the thinking of the Stefan George Circle, would have been *creative*.

Original (or creative) speech is a matter of making something apparent, which in turn is a matter of describing something as something. Gadamer's first example is technological: To understand something as a hammer means to understand it as a tool for hammering. We understand it in its what-is-it-for (*wozu*), an indirect reference on Gadamer's part to Heidegger's concept of *Zuhändenheit*.[7] The point here is that the understanding of a thing we are not now acquainted with is contingent upon having a logically prior point of view: We find ourselves in a workshop, we are presented with a thing never before seen, and we come to understand it in terms of what it does for us in the present context, in the *situatedness*, of the workshop. Original speech is like this: It seeks to understand things in terms of our interest, which is inseparable from our situatedness in this contingent world.[8]

Yet there is a more basic form of speech which is free of practical determination, and herein lies a deeper origin of *theoria*. That is to say, the description of the hammer we reviewed above was situationally determined, and therefore the speech was not really all that original or creative. Hence Gadamer, here following Heidegger, wants to push on to a more basic form of speech, one that is not already theory-laden because it is not practically situated. In making this move, Gadamer introduces one of the better-known terms of his mature philosophy, namely that of *play*. But in contrast to isolated exposition in *Truth and Method*, here it is put into a language context—its own peculiar form of *situatedness*—that helps us make sense of it.

Between tasks, in our moments of leisure—that is to say, in the suspension of practical situatedness—we are able to ask about things for their own sake, and hence from the outset our answers are not theoretically predetermined by practical needs. If I am correct in following out Gadamer's argument at

this point, he is claiming that truly *original* speech is a somewhat late arrival on the human scene. This is why I preferred
to call it *creative* a few paragraphs ago. Original, or creative
speech, comes only after practical needs have been tended to.
It comes with leisure, for only at this point is man freed of the
pressing situatedness of practical life. The character of this
modification, claims Gadamer, is indicated by an example,
namely *play*. Since Gadamer is here introducing a basic concept of his philosophical hermeneutics, it is worth our while to
quote him in full:

> The character of this modification will become clear
> in a special form of relaxation, that of the game. It is
> essential to games that the players are 'there,' which
> means that they let themselves be taken up by what
> is expected in the game without bearing in mind that
> the game is not serious. This is the case even though
> the game is for the purpose of recreation, that is, for the
> purpose of a later activity. Existence for the sake of the
> thing is therefore in playing actually neutral. It is not
> the thing, however much it must be taken seriously,
> that constitutes the purpose of the game. It is rather the
> mode of our being toward the thing, meaning that a
> thing is the object of concern and effort without being
> something which would be taken 'seriously' as the ob-
> ject of such care. The object of the playful effort is some-
> thing upon which nothing else depends: play itself is
> the reason for being of the game.[9]

Gadamer then goes on to draw his first understanding of
conversation from the model of the game. It is essential to real
conversation that someone else be there, another player, and
it is also essential that the conversation not be determined by
an outside practical interest. Indeed, it is in the nature of relaxed conversation to want to be with someone else and to
want to have that someone else, the Other, be a co-determi-
nant of the course of the conversation. That is to say, every

conversation partner seeks the agreement of the Other. This, Gadamer claims, is in the nature of conversation, and surely common sense would tell us that he is correct in this: A talk between two persons in which one does not seek the agreement of the other is anything but a conversation. It lacks the vital element of play that is constantly to be seen in our efforts to get the Other to agree by nodding, by contributing his experience, or even by disagreeing so that we know where he stands in respect to the final agreement that is sought. This is not to say that agreement must occur for a conversation to have taken place. We all have enough acrimony in conversations to recognize that agreement often is the last thing produced by conversation. Nonetheless, Gadamer seems on solid ground in arguing that the quest for agreement is in the nature of conversation.

It pays to pause at this point and give some shape to the term *conversation*. At times in his early writings, Gadamer clarifies his own meaning by using the adjective *philosophical* before the term *conversation*, and what he means by this is that the conversation is free of practical situatedness, or at least as free as it can be. But more often than not, Gadamer simply uses the German term for *conversation* without a qualifying adjective, and it has to be understood that he is assuming the suspension of practical situatedness. *Play*, therefore, characterizes human relationships that are not under the press of practical needs, and conversation is one form of this play.

Finally, the suspension of practical situatedness that is the condition of the possibility of play should not be misunderstood. The suspension does not amount to a denial of human situatedness itself but rather amounts to a denial (or satisfaction) of the needs of the human body and the peculiar situatedness imposed by those needs. In this respect, the term *practical* is as ambivalent in German as it is in English. On the one hand, it refers to activities like labor or work which are determined by the needs of the body. On the other hand, the term *practical* refers to activities like politics or philosophy which have to free themselves from bodily determinations in order to achieve their own being. A simple conversation or a philosophical conversation in Gadamer's early writings is an activity that has freed itself from practical bodily determinations in order to achieve its own free being. It ceases to take bodily needs seriously so that it can take itself seriously. As Plato in the *Parmenides* notes, play is finally a very serious thing.

Has Gadamer solved the problem with which he began? That is to say, has he shown why and how Aristotelian apodictic flows from Platonic dialectic? How can a mode of philosophical proceeding that requires no agreement flow from one that requires agreement? Even without Gadamer's argumentation, we can provide the answer, simply by recalling what he said in his 1927 piece on the Aristotelian *Protreptikos*. Gadamer then speculated that the Aristotelian text called *Protreptikos* was a disguised dialogue. The same is now the case: Aristotelian apodictic is really disguised—or rather, assumed—Platonic dialectic. It is not so much that Aristotle's arguments require no agreement. It is rather that the arguments proceed on the basis of agreements already arrived at. In this way, Gadamer provides a theory of philosophical development that is radically different from that of Werner Jaeger. We do well at this point to recall why this is the case.

Jaeger argued that Aristotle abandoned Plato's Idealism for a form of Realism that was vastly superior. In providing a developmental explanation, Jaeger inadvertently created a problem by inserting an epistemological break between Plato and Aristotle. Gadamer's solution does away with this break by arguing that Aristotle's science presupposes and takes advantage of the theoretical achievement of Plato. In other words, the Platonic dialogues are long, *playful* philosophical conversations aimed at reaching agreements on moral terms. Precisely because Plato's dialogues succeed so well, Aristotle is able to presuppose them and go on to seemingly much more monological and less playful argumentation of the *Nicomachean Ethics*. Aristotle is indeed an Aristotelian, but Aristotelianism is inconceivable without the prior success of Platonism.

This exciting argument, central to Gadamer's book, as its title indicates, can be restated in abstract but plain terms: Thinking begins in the leisurely, playful activity of the conversation because in playful conversation, thinking is not predetermined by practical needs. In this experience of *play*, inchoate experience is tossed back and forth and agreement is sought as to what it was that was experienced. This dialectical quest for moral terms, if successful, results in agreements which serve as the foundations for a subsequent form of argumentation that, apparently, requires no further agreement of a conversation partner. But it requires no further agreement only because that agreement has already been gained. If this argument can be accepted, then sense can be made of Gadamer's shorthand: not that Plato's ethics are dialectical but rather that Platonic dialectics are ethical. Ethics, as the creation by the free man of moral standards for this life, begins in the free association of the imagination.

This argument can be restated as a description of *thinking* itself. If I sit back and think about thinking, the first conclusion I might reach is that thinking is a private affair and what I then vocalize in public is a consequence of this private affair. The public sphere is thus an extension of the private sphere, according to this argument. But if I reflect just a moment longer, it should occur to me that thinking itself, this seemingly private affair, is a conversation I am having with myself, and if I reflect on that internal conversation, I should quickly recognize that all the arguments I make to myself are arguments I have to varying degrees read or heard from someone else. Even reading, which at first seems so private, is really a public affair. It is obviously a conversation with someone else, someone not present, but nonetheless someone. Now according to this argumentation, the public precedes the private, and indeed the private activity of thinking is really not at all private. What we call *thinking* is really internalized conversation, and like all conversation, requires the agreement of the partners. It requires the agreement of me with myself, and this is the most fundamental form of friendship.

The virtue of this argument in the young Gadamer's writings is that it is not at all vague or half-baked. He may not draw some of the conclusions I have drawn here, but he gets right to the essence of all these questions with his concept of *play*. For it is this concept that enables us to distinguish a real conversation from a pseudo-conversation. Also, by sketching in the concept of *play* in opposition to the imperatives of practical, bodily needs, Gadamer gives us an absolutely primary justification for leisure, education, theory, and a class of persons—apart from the working class—who will enjoy these benefits.

III

In the third section, called "The Shared-World Motiv of Substantiality," the mood of Gadamer's habilitation thesis shifts dramatically. To this point, Gadamer has been writing about Plato, orienting his interpretations toward a dialogue theory of Plato's writings, and establishing that science is not a theoretical restatement of what is in fact the case but was rather originally a conversation aimed at establishing the theory that would in turn enable facts to be cognized in the first place and then re-cognized. Now suddenly the focus shifts and becomes contemporary. Gadamer now wants to analyze what really goes into conversation and consequently is willing to drop away the classical philosophical scaffolding and discuss conversation as such.

Up to this point, Gadamer has used a somewhat mysterious reference to *the Other* as an element in any conversation.[10] Now the Other begins to take shape as the ideal conversation partner and hence takes on a vital importance. Gadamer now gives vent to his own talents and gives this Other shape by means of a delightful juggling of his German terms. In doing so, Gadamer shows a keen appreciation of the power of word-play.[11] He introduces a game in which his wit shows his awareness that words always have multiple meanings and that the right word in the wrong context or vice versa can virtually compel the Other in a conversation to participate by making the desirable adjustments. In this case, Gadamer is not trying to be funny. He is rather trying to show that the key components of conversation all have to do with language and speech.

It is difficult and sometimes impossible to translate Gadamer's wordplay into English without losing its underlying message, so I shall install the German term immediately after the English as soon as it appears. As already noted, the basic German terms Gadamer uses relate to language and speech, and they play off each other either because they rhyme or because they are nearly identical. Since Gadamer often uses the pronoun *I* to refer to the Other's conversation partner, I shall follow him in this too. But let me first list the words Gadamer employs in his wordplay:

sprechen	(to speak)
Gespräch	(conversation)
ansprechen	(to address)
widersprechen	(to contradict)
Anspruch	(claim)
entsprechen	(to correspond)
stimmen	(to voice, to agree)
zustimmen	(to agree to)
übereinstimmen	(to agree)
Stimmung	(mood)

Now Gadamer: when the *I* has a conversation, he is engaging in a *Gespräch*, the literal meaning of which is "from speech," a meaning which cannot be heard out of the English "conversation" but is clear in the German *Ge-spräch*, if we insert a dash and pause at that point. It is also clear from this term that the *I* engaged in conversation will find himself speaking, since *Gespräch* is derived from *sprechen*, which means "to speak." Now, in speaking conversationally, the *I* will necessarily "address" himself to another. There is no other way to have a conversation except by addressing someone. The applicable German term here is *ansprechen*, meaning literally "to speak to." Then, to complete our initial sketch, this conversation will only work if the other corresponds to the *I* in conversational ability, and the term for correspond in this sense of a balanced or equal ability is *entsprechen*, which literally means to "speak from." The ideal of balance is an important one in Gadamer's theory of conversation, for without it nothing can be achieved.

What the *I* seeks from the Other in conversation is "agreement," and the German term Gadamer uses is *zustimmen*, which literally translated means "to voice," the word for which is *stimmen*. An "agreement" is a *Zustimmung*, or a conclusion to which one has "voiced" approval. Or alternatively, what is sought in conversation is *Übereinstimmung*, which literally means achieving "one voice above" the conversation. It also suggests achieving a different "mood," the German term for which is *Stimmung*. Therefore, agreement must be freely given, or otherwise it is incapable of achieving the new, higher mood. Hence I must be willing to allow my conversation partner to contradict me, and here the German term is *widersprechen*, which literally means "to speak against." But the contradiction should not be simply arbitrary. It rather takes on the form of a new argument, and hence it begins with a claim, the German term for which is *Anspruch*, a term which derives from *ansprechen*, or "to speak to." At this point we come full circle, for now the *I* is being addressed and its agreement is sought. The conversational process starts all over again, but the aim remains the same: to achieve the new and higher mood of shared agreement.

This is obviously a highly abstract description of what a conversation is, and if we are to characterize it in a single word appropriate to the thinking of the German 1920s, then that word would be *Mitwelt*.[12] In translating the section title, I have deviated from the conventional translation of *Mitwelt* as "one's contemporaries" and translated this term literally as "shared-world," but it cannot be simply altered in this way without trying to grasp its significance. Above all, the term refers to a social ideal, namely the ideal of community (*Gemeinschaft*) which has for so long fascinated Germans, and it stands opposed to the negative utopia of society (*Gesellschaft*), which represents the anomic, anarchic state that modernization had brought Germany to. These terms had been introduced into German academic discourse by Ferdinand Tönnies, the sociologist. In Gadamer's case, there is a considerable narrowing from the normal use of the term *Mitwelt*. Gadamer is not trying to identify the ideal community as such. He is rather trying to identify the ideal *philosophical* community, and this of course is considerably less than the universal ideal.

The brief and playful discussion of the Other's characteristics as a conversation partner is a prelude to discussing the most basic corruption of the *Mitwelt*, the ideal philosophical community.[13] According to Gadamer, the fall from grace occurs because speech always says more than it intends. That is to say, overt verbal speech is always accompanied by a language of gesture, and this may communicate an entirely different message than the one intended. Normally, the language of gesture is more accurate in portraying one's self (as opposed to what one is talking about) because it is involuntary and hence, supposedly, more natural (and objective) than speech. Therefore the outcome of a conversation can be skewed one way or another by this underlying text. Ideally what Gadamer wants to identify is scientific speech, and hence he seeks to exclude the underlying text carried by the language of gesture. He urges, insofar as it is possible, that there be a disregard (*Absehen*) from this subtext of gesture, thereby protecting the pure verbal argument from the dangers posed by flattery, muted hostility, or—as in the case of the not-so-muted hostility of Thrasymachus in the first book of the *Republic*—outright fuming rage. The Platonic Socrates is clearly able to disregard this subtext.

Gadamer next makes a move which widens the scope of the discussion considerably.[14] Until now, he has been talking about a conversation in the conventional sense of the term. If the conversation is ideal, then the Other is not really an individual who will intrude himself into a conversation. He is rather arguing against something, not against someone. Now this kind of ideal Other—ideal because he is the embodiment of pure reason—can be replaced, and we should be clear as to why this is the case. The individual who is expressing himself—his hostility or his joy or whatever—is unique in the contours of his personality and his argument. But the Other who is simply hearing and responding to an argument with a counterargument is doing something that any number of other well-trained thinkers could do. For this reason, he can be replaced or, as now becomes clear in Gadamer's presentation, displaced.

What has been conversation in an external sense of the term now becomes internalized, and this, as I have already indicated in the comments on Aristotle's apodictic, is what Gadamer calls *thinking*. That is to say, thinking is an internal conversation of the self with its Other. This is what I meant when I said that the Other could be "displaced." It can be internalized. The function of the now-internalized *Other* is to correspond to the *I*, to listen to the claims of the *I*, to answer them with agreement, if they are respectably argued, or with counterclaims if they are not. And to the extent that the *I* is turned into the listener of the Other's counterclaims, he is turned into a sort of "Other." The distinction between I and Other now gradually begins to break down, and we become less aware that thinking is originally a conversation. The two worlds, those of the I and the Other, now begin to become a real *Mitwelt* of thinking.

At this point, Gadamer takes the opportunity to argue his own point against that of his friend and colleague Karl Löwith.[15] In his own habilitation thesis, also done for Heidegger, Löwith had argued that *thinking* was, to use Gadamer's words, the "mere spinning out of solid presuppositions and a mere logic of consequences. . . ." Gadamer noted that he wanted to emphasize that Löwith's analysis was "one-sided," but in doing so Gadamer also said a good deal about his own putatively two-sided analysis. Gadamer had wanted to focus his habilitation thesis on the idealistic notion of a *Mitwelt*, and in doing so, he gave in slightly to the temptation to treat Löwith's argument as a strawman. The title of Löwith's habilitation thesis may be loosely translated as "The Individual in the Roll of the Ideal Other" (*Das Individuum in der Rolle des Mitmenschen*), and it alone indicates that Löwith was dealing with the problem of how a *Mitwelt* could possibly emerge from a society filled with bourgeois individuals. The extent to which Löwith lost sight of the ideal of the *Mitwelt* and took up *das Individuum* as his own ideal is difficult to assess, but Gadamer's criticism is based on his own judgment that this is in fact what happened.[16]

IV

Yet Gadamer's criticism of Löwith was not gratuitous. Although relegated to a footnote, it was part of an analysis that Gadamer had already initiated and which he intended to continue. This was the analysis of the corruption of conversation and, we might now add, the corruption of thinking due to the intrusion of the subtext of the individual's personality. This corruption, or *Fall*, as Gadamer puts it, now becomes Gadamer's major theme.[17]

By introducing the term *Fall*, Gadamer gives an indication of the extent to which his own categories are neither modern nor classical but rather biblical, and it might be appropriate here to briefly sketch the problem involved with biblical cate-

gories in a language philosophy. The notion of a *Fall* entails
the existence of a prior state in which language—or in Gadamer's case, conversation—was perfect. In the Bible, the Ada-
mic language spoken in the Garden of Eden is apparently perfect because it was in exact correspondence with the animals
Adam names. In Gadamer, conversation was supposedly perfect because the partners held to Socratic rules, such as the
profession of ignorance, etc. In the Bible, the Fall comes with
the introduction of sin, and it is seemingly irreversible. Thereafter everything is babel, so to speak. In Gadamer's case, the
Fall took place with the rise of sophism, and whether it was or
was not irreversible is a basic question of Platonic philosophy
or, rightly understood, of philosophy itself.

Much of German philology in the nineteenth century was
structured in and perhaps determined by biblical categories.
That is to say, it was presupposed without argumentation that
there was a single, perfect speech in the beginning. This sort
of linguistics is most often associated with the work of Franz
Bopp and Jakob Grimm, following the breakthrough made by
Sir William Jones with his claims for Sanskrit as a *mother
tongue*. The device of the *language tree*, for example, is a revealing rhetorical figure in that it presupposes a single trunk
from which all present languages are the branches. The aim of
such an effort was often to establish human brotherhood or, as
is suggested with the term *Indo-Germanic*, to refer to the lost
original mother language (before Sanskrit) and also to suggest
Germany's cultural pedigree among the European countries.
There were of course philologists who argued that different
languages or language families had purely local origins, an
argument that would fit in very nicely with the Heideggerian
claim that we are restricted by our circumstances in time and,
presumably, place. But these linguistic relativists, as they
would come to be called in the twentieth century, did not sit at
center stage in the linguistics of the nineteenth century.

The use of the term *Fall* by Gadamer in his habilitation
thesis is potentially very damaging to Gadamer's case, for it
suggests that he believes there was a Socratic Garden of Eden

in which all participants were in perfect agreement and that sophist vanity got in the way to spoil this philosophical utopia. His vocabulary, it would seem, determines Gadamer toward a kind of linguistic foundationalism, to finding his way back to a scene in which perfect conversations were carried out. Or to put this matter into a distinctly Germanic form, such a concept as that of a Fall inclines Gadamer to a vision in which a perfect *Gemeinschaft*, or interpretive community, came first, followed by the atomized *Gesellschaft*, or mass society, led by the Sophists. Yet within Platonic philosophy, it was the Sophists who were there at the outset, and it was in respect to this problem and the modified babel of the first book of Plato's *Republic* that Socrates set out to do battle.

In Gadamer's case, the term *Fall* need not be taken seriously at all. If anything, it is a habitual form, perhaps adopted unthinkingly, but signifying nothing insofar as the vocabulary is not accompanied by the expected argumentation. It corresponds to a certain ambiguity in Plato—namely, the notion of recollection of a life, more ideal than that of the present, once lived—but this is not a possibility that Gadamer shows any inclination to take seriously. In Gadamer's presentation, the notion of a Fall is rather used to provide an umbrella over arguments that Plato was making in specific texts. In the *Sophist*, the *Laws*, and the *Seventh Letter*, Plato characterizes the substantive spirit of conversational understanding in identical terms: Plato's concern, according to Gadamer, is with the exclusion of *phthonos*, or jealousy, which designates the imbalance that results in the Other being either slightly ahead or slightly behind the I in conversation. In this argument, Gadamer's reading of Plato strongly implies that there was once a situation of *aphthonos*, a certain balance in which the conversation flowed smoothly because all sides were intellectually equal. This can only refer to a situation of professed ignorance of putatively objective ethical principles, for only at such a point can true ethical activity take its beginning. At such a point, it is clear that dialectics themselves are ethical because nothing is being privileged. It is the situation of privileged knowledge claims that Plato would exclude, and he would exclude them in favor of a new beginning.

The essence of sophism is to take advantage of and, indeed, expand the situation dominated by *phthonos*. Not only do the sophists make privileged language claims, but it is their intent in conversation to silence the Other. Sophist monologue is therefore not simply an accidental characteristic of the way the Sophists go about redeeming their knowledge claims. It is rather a characteristic of an atomized social situation which is anything but democratic. It is this "fallen" situation that Plato would reverse. It is therefore that the *Platonic Socrates* is created as the personification of the virtues of the perfect philosophical conversation.

V

The *Platonic Socrates* is treated by Gadamer in the fifth section, entitled "The Socratic Dialogue," as the personification of the theory of dialectic.[18] That is to say, the Platonic Socrates is treated as an ideal type, and what Gadamer is looking for in his effort to reconstitute the theory of dialogue is the presuppositions that are given in the Socratic effort to reach an understanding with the Other with whom he is conversing. This personification is best explained by an example.

At issue in any Socratic dialogue is *knowledge*, and part of the problem of reconstituting a productive dialogue is being clear about what this term intends. The opponents of Socrates presuppose knowledge to be a positivistic thing, which is to say that they presuppose a preexistent reality which can be known piecemeal and finally, through the accumulation of piecemeal knowledge, as a whole. But this kind of positivistic knowledge, given that it exists, is irrelevant to what Socrates seeks. For positivistic knowledge is something that one may have or not have to live an ethical life, says Gadamer. I, for example, may not have a knowledge of the techniques that go into the production of steel, and I as an ethical being may get along quite well without such knowledge. Or I may not have a knowledge of medicine but can get along without it as an ethical being. But there is one kind of knowledge which everyone—the steelworker and the physician as well as I—must have in order to be considered human beings at all. This is moral knowledge, and it is the knowledge Socrates seeks.

It belongs to the being of man, Gadamer argues, to understand what man is in his virtue. This is not to say that one must at this very moment have a clear idea of what virtue is, but one must at least seek to find out what it is, else one is not a (civilized) man. Hence in the *Protagorus* it is argued that it is a form of madness to fail to claim that one is just, and similar arguments may be found in the *Charmenides* and the *Gorgias*, according to Gadamer.[19] These fragmentary arguments then set the stage for the .imperative quality of the argument pursued in the *Republic*. Hence at this point, in his interpretation of Plato, Gadamer is making a very strong claim, indeed, a universality claim: Man is an ethical being, and this means that he is a thinking and knowing being. A knowledge and understanding of the *Good* is therefore absolutely necessary to *human* being. In contrast, a knowledge of technological realities and possibilities is not necessary (although it may be desirable) to the leading of a distinctly human life. Man is not, by virtue of his nature as man, a technological being. But man is, by nature, an ethical being.

In other words, to be a citizen is to live with others in a community, and one necessarily must claim that one is just if one is a citizen. There is a certain irreducible necessity to this position and Gadamer finds it compelling. Even the criminal, if he is not out of his mind, will claim to have been acting according to some concept of justice. To claim that one is *un*just and mean it in more than a rebellious or irrational sense is conceivable but highly unlikely. Even Adolf Hitler, presumably, believed he was doing the just thing when he exterminated the Jews. It is this that makes even Hitler still a human being and, therefore, still an object of our moral judgment. But then if even the most misled human being does claim to be just, then he or his lawyer (one of them is a potential conversation partner) must be prepared to answer the question of why such and such an action was just. One must be prepared to argue, to use language, and thereby to participate in the constitution of the *polis*. So argues Gadamer, and at this point it becomes clear why politics is a philosophic necessity and why the *Seventh Letter* must be deemed authentic. Man is, by his peculiar nature, the animal that speaks, and the reason man speaks is to seek out of the variety of human action a common moral denominator.

This is the first presupposition of Socratic argumentation. When put into practice, it leads immediately to a conclusion: Socrates' contemporaries—his *Mitwelt* in the conventional usage of that term—do not satisfy this requirement. Put more bluntly, there is no such thing as a Platonic dialogue in which the Other conversing with Socrates is able to adequately argue a moral philosophy. Everyone claims he is just, but no one can explain why. What is argued is the ruling understanding of justice, or to put this into Gadamer's later terminology, the prejudices of the times are argued, and for the best of young men, these prejudices are never adequate. They thus lead to doubt, and doubts about the justice of a specific action leads finally to doubt about justice itself. We have to be careful at this point to be clear that Gadamer is not saying that an action is unjust if it cannot be argued. He is rather saying that even a just action will be counterproductive to the norms of the community if no one can argue why it is just in terms of a shared concept of justice.

Gadamer then continues by arguing that the resulting skepticism, especially in young men, will lead to the rise of *hedonism* as an alternative to the argumentatively inadequate but still prevailing social norms. The reason that hedonism is attractive to young men is that it substitutes very nicely for argument. Indeed, it performs more efficiently than any philosophical argument. The attraction of hedonism, according to Gadamer, is that it offers an immediate rather than a mediated relationship between everday action and the Good. Our initial reaction on consuming a piece of home-baked cake is to say something like: "It tastes *good*." The reaction is unmediated. It is beyond question, and this means that it is beyond argument. It is the directness and immediacy of hedonism as opposed to the indirectness and constantly mediated philosophical pursuit of the (Idea of the) Good that give hedonism its strongest appeal.

The situation now created calls upon Socrates to engage in questioning aimed at refutation of hedonism, and Gadamer makes clear that the purpose of the effort is to establish a philosophical *Mitwelt* with the conversational Other.[20] That is to say, Socratic questioning is aimed at demonstrating the real moral ignorance of his knowing contemporary, thereby equalizing the two conversation partners, insofar as Socrates has already professed moral ignorance. When viewed from this perspective, Socratic irony and other techniques of refutation all appear as part of a grand scheme. They are aimed at destroying the foundationalism of hedonism for the sake of giving birth to an authentic practical philosophy.

At this point Gadamer can introduce the *Idea of the Good* as a central theme of Platonic philosophizing and, one might add, of his own life's work in philosophy. Perhaps because this is an introduction or, perhaps, because this is a habilitation thesis which will have to be defended before a board of academic examiners, Gadamer is as precise as he will ever be in defining his notion of the *Idea of the Good* and making it cohere with all that he has said thus far. But before reviewing Gadamer's argument, it should be stressed that he is not speaking of the Good as such but rather of the *Idea* of the Good. Now given what has been claimed in this book about the denial of a doctrine of objective ideas in Plato, we are in a good position to anticipate that the Idea of the Good is basically a claim, the purpose of which is to give philosophical argument a starting point. Gadamer, or rather Gadamer's Plato, does not know what the Good is, but he most certainly has a prejudice about it.

The Idea of the Good, Gadamer argues, has the general character of a what's-it-about (*wozu*) of human existence.[21] That is to say, it identifies a central defining purpose of distinctly human activity, a *logos kath' auto* or universal (moral) concept, to use the language of Aristotle. In this understanding of self, not just my self but self in general, the human being is given a point of reference, a place to take a stand, an opportunity to locate all actions not simply in terms of the pleasure they give but also and more so in terms of what they contribute to the attainment of the human being that does not yet exist, first formulated in the Idea of the Good. This general sense of the Good is already apparent, according to Gadamer, in the *Protagorus*, where Socrates is able to compel his conversation partner to make a unified presentation of his understanding of human existence.[22] He will then use this standard, the Idea of the Good generally stated by Socrates's conversation partner, as the standard in his refutation of the self-same opponent.

The Idea of the Good seeks its own authentic good, which is the realization of the human self, and this can never be the product of the immediate good provided by the pursuit of hedonistic good. The reason is that the immediate good or pleasure experienced by the senses can always turn into a subsequent Bad, or painful experience. There is no stability in pleasure. Therefore no real human self can be the consequence of it. Thus for Gadamer, the Idea of the Good emerges as a constant possibility of realizing the self, admittedly ideal. Actions that are pleasant in their immediate consequences can be repressed, those which are immediately painful—such as dying for one's country—can be willingly undertaken, if they can be justified in terms of this Idea of the Good.

The Idea of the Good thus finally offers a standard of *measure* that enables ethics to become something of a science, and it is on precisely this basis that it demonstrates that it is a real knowledge in place of the seeming knowledge of hedonism. A standard of any type must be detached from the matter that it is measuring, but hedonism's standard of measure—immediate gratification of the senses—is not at all detached from the experience it is measuring. The Platonic Idea of the Good, in contrast, is detached, and this enables it to act to scientifically measure life's pleasures and pains. So finally what is revealed in Gadamer's presentation is that there is no necessary conflict between the Platonic Idea of the Good and the pleasures of everyday existence. If anything, the opposite is the case. The Idea of the Good, if properly used, can ensure the optimum possible pleasure, something which hedonism, with its emphasis on immediacy, can never do. But this, we should be clear, is the pleasure of an ideal self brought to the highest degree of achievement possible.

No doubt Gadamer's initial approach to the topic of the Idea of the Good is keyed to locating this term in Plato, but what stands out in Gadamer's juxtapositioning of the Platonic Idea of the Good with hedonism is a mode of thinking characteristic of modern German romanticism. Key to the construction of modern German romanticism in the late eighteenth century was the sensationalism of Locke and the materialism of the French Enlightenment, and the charge against them was not so much that they were mistaken but that Lockean sensationalism provides no focus to the human mind. Mind responds to whatever has an impact on it, and the result is a willy-nilly construction of the human mind or, if nature has an orderly structure, a mind whose order is not its own but is rather that of a mysterious nature outside us.

Hedonism functions in much the same way. There is no logic to the pleasures presented by nature. They are, as we like to say, very much a matter of *taste*, pulling human beings in one direction, then another, leading to nothing in particular beyond the "good" of the moment. Culture thus remains at something of a standstill, never getting beyond the tastes of the moment. Within an organized society, control over tastes can be gained and held as long as one remains aware of some of the natural laws of taste, such as the law of diminishing marginal returns. One taste succeeds the next and, hence, fashion predominates.

The German romantic response to this situation was to emphasize the *self*. Better: It emphasized *consciousness* as the mode of gaining access to the self, and language as the means of putting the self into an objectified position from which it could be "read" by human beings. In other words, German romanticism reinvented or rediscovered the classical formula for humanism: It relearned how to provide a model, or *Gestalt*, of human imitation. Concretely, the cutting edge of romantic humanism was seen to be the literary canon, or rather those pieces of established literature that were to be recommended to the attention of young people because of the potential they had for shaping a desirable *self*. In this context, the struggle for control of the Prussian and later German *Gymnasium* in the nineteenth century was a struggle for the control of the German mind, ultimately a struggle for control of the German *self*.

The Romantics represented an Idea of the Good, of the ideal *self*, and concretely this took shape as a canon of classical Greek literary texts. The members of the Stefan George Circle brought this romantic inclination to its sharpest formulation with their creation of the genre of *Gestalt*-biographies. As opposed to this romantic tendency, an industrializing Germany emphasized the alternative self of scientific man. Increasingly, as industrialization took shape and Germany appeared irrevocably committed to that course, the tendency of universities was to make physicists, chemists, biologists, and mathematicians out of young Germans. It was a different idea of the self, one that was given to the immediate pleasures of the products of industrial civilization. Gadamer's position was clear. He represented the Romantic notion that the educational establishment needed a clear picture or *Bild* of the whole self for it to proceed in an effective fashion.

At this point, Gadamer's consideration of the *Platonic Socrates* concludes, and so too does Gadamer's theoretical argument. He is now ready to go on to other works of Plato and finally to a detailed consideration of the *Philebos*, a text which Gadamer takes to be an exercise in the internalized dialogue of moral thinking. This is to say that the dialogue that takes place in the *Philebos* is between the *I* and its possible *Other*, but in the case of the *Philebos*, they are one and the same person, namely, the Platonic Socrates.

VI

In concluding on Gadamer's habilitation thesis, we do well to make things less rather than more complicated. That is to say, up to now I have attempted to reconstruct and unpack Gadamer's dense argumentation, and at this point we do well to simplify that argumentation for the sake of understanding. Hence I will attempt to focus on one theme—namely, the character of philosophy—and see how well this thread can be woven through all that Gadamer has said.

Philosophy has become a problem in the twentieth century due to the status of *knowledge* claims and how they are treated. The problem is not with knowledge as a goal or as a fact of life but rather with the kind of status knowledge is given in a discipline that also, at least since Socrates, claims to be about *thinking*. Regardless of what specific shape knowledge actually has, what distinguishes it and makes it problematic for thinking is that it claims to be a foundation for thinking, and insofar as knowledge succeeds in establishing itself in this foundational role, it is not only placing itself beyond the determination of thinking, it is also making itself into the determinant of thinking.

We get a concrete anticipation of the problem I am pointing to if we look at the subfield of sociology called *sociology of knowledge*. This subfield would not have arisen if academics and, more generally, modern social structure, had not privileged knowledge over thinking and thereby created one of the conditions of the material prosperity of the intellectual class. The acquisition and control of knowledge as a means of production has been richly rewarded with money, status, and influence in modern industrial societies, and thinking as a pure activity, uncontaminated by acquisitive desires, has everywhere had a relatively difficult time. Therefore—that is, because knowledge was highly privileged and thinking not so privileged—what gradually took shape in modern industrial societies were social classes which distinguished themselves by virtue of their control of certain forms of knowledge. Modern universities, in other words, tend to be populated by *savants* rather than thinkers.

It is this unargued premise, which I take to be for the most part correct, that is behind such a book as Fritz Ringer's *The Decline of the German Mandarins*.[23] The premise is also at work in Thomas Kuhn's *Structure of Scientific Revolutions*, where it takes the form of "normal science" (the knowledge class) and "revolutionary science" (the thinking class).[24] My specific point is that Gadamer's early work also makes sense in terms of this distinction between thinking and knowledge which, like the distinction between speaking cultures and writing cultures, is originally an attempt to break down the mind of a civilization whose intellectual life has become frozen.

Put differently, the problem is a matter of *privilege*. All claims made in philosophy are nothing more than the beginning points of argumentation, and the hoped-for conclusion is the reaching of an agreement, that which Gadamer calls an understanding. This is something that is admittedly less than the establishment of an absolute underpinning of knowledge. But if a claim is privileged as "knowledge," then it is set outside the framework of dialogue, as happens whenever anyone begins a conversation with the words, "As we all know . . . ," or "As everyone knows . . . ," or "Of course . . . ," or "Naturally . . . ," or "Obviously. . . ." These are all attempts, seemingly harmless and not worth boorish objection, to privilege a small area of agreement as being beyond argumentative discussion and hence capable of serving as a determinant, when needed.

The most privileged positions in philosophy are occupied not by the opinionated upstarts we encounter in daily conversation but rather the seemingly impeccable foundations or unchallenged claims of the established natural sciences. The popular notion that the natural sciences constitute the "hard" sciences or the "exact" sciences already makes it likely that conclusions reached in these sciences will be privileged as *knowledge* rather than taken as mere *thinking* and will, hence, be available as determinants in philosophical conversation. Thus any effort to deprivilege philosophical claims based on the natural sciences is especially difficult because they have strong popular backing in the modern world.

In fact, unless a science is conducted in an inexact and sloppy manner, there is only one way to deprivilege the major conclusions of the exact natural sciences. This is to claim and argue that their conclusions, although hard and exact as claimed, are dependent upon a certain point of view, and if this point of view—or *paradigm*, in Kuhn's language—is altered, then a different and equally valid set of conclusions may be arrived at. If one presupposes the geocentric hypothesis, then methods based on empirical analysis, carefully executed, will work to demonstrate that the geocentric presupposition is correct: The sun does appear to go around the world. Of course, if one presupposes the heliocentric hypothesis, then the same empirical tools can be used to provide evidence that the opposite is the case: It is entirely possible, even necessary, to imagine the modern intellectual as someone who "sees" that the earth goes around the sun. Nowhere in the modern world does *theory determine fact* more dramatically than in this seventeenth-century argument among proponents of the geocentric and heliocentric hypotheses.

The point here is not to attack science or its achievements. They are the crowning glory of modern intellectual life. The point is rather to demonstrate that science and its achievements are initially based on *opinion* rather than knowledge. However painfully, we have come to learn that Darwin started with a point of view and that this was not the same as knowledge. Darwin then climbed a ladder, similar in structure to the "line" described at the end of the sixth book of Plato's *Republic*, leading gradually to agreement that the theory of natural selection provides an adequate framework for determining our view of life on this planet. Darwinian *knowledge* is thus not something that predated Darwin. It is rather an achievement, the consequence of argumentation and evidence. It seems to be in the nature of all great scientific theories that they come to be taken for granted and thereby gain an atemporal and unsituated aura that belies their situated historical origins. It is at this moment that a point of view gets privileged as knowledge: It is no longer something that is determined by human effort but is rather something that claims the right to be a determinant of human effort. At this point the relationship between thinking and knowledge has been stood on its head: Knowledge, the offspring of thinking, claims now to be the parent. At this point, the chief concern of philosophy ought to be to save itself by questioning the privileged position of knowledge.

Gadamer's position is much narrower, but its direction is basically the same as the one I am suggesting above. The privileged position is that of the *Realism* of Aristotle, and Gadamer's argument was initially aimed at depriviledging that position. At this point, I do not want to slip and have the early Gadamer making the strong claim that reality does not exist. I rather want to argue, alongside the early Gadamer, that philosophy distinguishes itself from science only because it does not presuppose the existence of reality. Pure philosophy rather presupposes nothing at all, and thus positions itself to recognize itself as pure theory, or a matter of words, as, for example, in the case of Plato's city in speech. Thereby, and only thereby, does it avoid positivism, for positivism—defined as the accumulation of raw data, brute facts, so that patterns can reveal themselves on their own natural terms—is not possible without the privileging of a reality that is beyond question.

Gadamer's argument in his early writings is, in my opinion, on the right track. That is to say, he is not solely dealing with the academic problem of explaining Aristotle's break with his master. At a deeper level, Gadamer is arguing that the positivistic quality of science, and of Aristotle, is originally based on a set of agreements, now taken to be commonplaces, first worked out in dialogue. Aristotelian ethical science, which provides answers, originates in Platonic ethical (moral) thinking, which raises questions. Aristotle is a magnificent moral philosopher, but this is not because he broke with Plato. On the contrary, it is because he stood on the shoulders of the Platonic achievement and, probably for reasons of intellectual economy, presupposed it.

This argument thoroughly refutes *Realism*, for whatever else Realism is, it represents a set of privileged (or presupposed) first principles from which one argues logically. Gadamer does not make the mistake of attacking in midstream, that is to say, attacking Aristotle's logic. He rather attacks where it counts, and that is at the point where privilege is being tacitly accorded, that is to say, where something is being put beyond argument. Implicitly, Gadamer finds himself arguing the most radical of philosophical positions. This is that if philosophy is to really be philosophy, it must question *every* privilege accorded by mind. It cannot tolerate a single one, for philosophy *as such* is absolutely defeated by the intrusion of even a single privilege. Philosophy is absolute argument or it is not philosophy.

This formulation is only seemingly radical. Why, one might ask, cannot philosophy retain *some* privileged positions, as long as it eliminates most? How, in fact, can philosophy happen at all unless some positions are privileged, so that a stand can be taken? Indeed, how can an argument take place at all unless the I or the Other making the argument privileges some position as being true and hence worthy of the effort that goes into argument? Does not an absolute deprivileging of every position threaten philosophy itself with the anarchy of relativism? These questions are not trivial, for they remind us that philosophy, too, is a finite human activity. It cannot create *ex nihilo* but must rather have some material which is beyond question.

In his fashion, Gadamer answers all these familiar questions in his treatment of Plato. First of all, by arguing that Plato's ethics are dialectical, Gadamer means to say that they do not privilege any single position but rather submit all positions, including the position of the Platonic Socrates, to argumentative scrutiny. Plato is not an *Idealist* standing opposed to the *Realist* Aristotle for the simple reason that Plato does not privilege ideas. Following the thinking of Paul Natorp, which by 1928 had become so domesticated to Gadamer's mind that it was used without acknowledgment, Gadamer takes Plato's ideas to be *hypotheses*, positions put forward not as truths but rather as propositions to be tested. There is no better example of this than the *Idea of the Good* as it is treated in Gadamer's habilitation thesis. Gadamer comes perilously close, so it would seem, to privileging this idea. In any case, there is no other ethical idea that is even argued in Gadamer's habilitation thesis, and the Idea of the Good is argued with an intent to give it a defining position in ethics. Indeed, Gadamer even goes so far as to argue that it is a standard of measure for conduct, and this seems to be putting it into the unshakeable position of a judge.

But close examination of Gadamer's text shows that even this position is finally dialectical. Gadamer, in the name of Plato, is not simply asserting, and thereby privileging, the Idea of the Good as an objective, Platonic idea. He is arguing it, and moreover he is arguing it against the appeals of hedonism as a standard for judging human activity. The case for hedonism is in fact made, as is the case for the Idea of the Good, and in the end Gadamer himself does not draw a definitive conclusion but rather leaves it to the reader to do that. Indeed, if we recall Gadamer's 1927 argument about the role of the concept of *mixing* in Plato, there is every reason to argue, as I did, that Plato did not intend the Idea of the Good as a device to exclude the pleasures that hedonism celebrates. He intended rather that the Idea of the Good be a standard for choosing among everyday pleasures so as to maximize human pleasure as such. This is a subtle argument, but if it is grasped correctly, it will be seen to be pulling the rug out from under hedonism by arguing hedonism's own main point. A life led according to the Idea of the Good will yield more, not less, pleasure than a life led according to the immediate gratification of the senses favored by hedonism.

If there is a privileging of anything in Gadamer's position, it is not the Idea of the Good but rather the Idea of Politics. Yet even here, if the argument is unfolded, it will be seen that Gadamer is not arbitrarily asserting the primacy of a preexisting thing called *politics* but is rather urging the primacy of the philosophical way of life in argumentative terms. Gadamer takes the autobiographical comments of the questionably authentic *Seventh Letter* to be authentic not for any of the reasons that would appeal to a professional philologist but rather because they fit in with an argument being made in Plato's unquestionably authentic texts. Plato's philosophy could not have been the antipolitical thing it is sometimes said to be without sacrificing its essential dialectical character. To argue that Plato's philosophy is antipolitical is tantamount to arguing that Plato and his followers were initiates into the Socratic mysteries and that they concocted a theory of the state that would make the philosopher into a king for the simple but grotesque reason of protecting their own privileges. True, the actual fate of Socrates and the repeated suggestions in the *Republic* that the philosopher will be put on trial and perhaps executed let on that Plato was aware of the possibility that the motivation of the philosophical exercise would be misunderstood. But we, following Plato and Gadamer, need not believe the charge against Socrates. We can set things aright by recognizing that it was the existing state that was on trial. Politics is hardly put beyond question in this format.

5

Ethics, Phronesis, and the Idea of the Good

I

One can easily distort Gadamer's early writings by reading them from the point of view of his later writings, thereby focusing on language to the exclusion of most everything else. I have already done some of this and will continue to do it, but it is also worth while to recall that the main theme of Gadamer's early writings is not so much language as it is ethics in the classical, politically related sense. We run the risk of cheating ourselves of a potentially rewarding harvest if we do not periodically come back to this more obvious thread and develop it for its own sake. Thus before looking at "Plato and the Poets" and "Plato's Educational State" from the point of view of language theorizing, I would like to locate Gadamer's ethical theorizing.

The term *ethics* is notoriously difficult to define. In fact, if we do actually succeed in defining the term, we may have already defeated our purpose by narrowing its scope too much. It is likely to lose its popular base in ordinary language and be remade into an academically manageable, logically rigorous category called *moral philosophy*. This indeed is what professional philosophers normally do, and it is to Gadamer's credit that he avoids this kind of winnowing. As I argued in the Preface to this book, Gadamer thereby shows his thinking to be nicely aligned with that of Max Weber in the latter's essay called "Politics as a Vocation."[1]

Weber argued against what he called a "perfectionist ethics" (*Gesinnungsethik*) and on behalf of what he called an "ethics of responsibility" (*Verantwortungsethik*).[2] In doing this, Weber successfully reasserted a basic insight about politics, namely, that it has no privileged moral "truths" which it can impose from above upon people. Therefore politics cannot be narrowed to an ideology or academic specialty without losing something vital. Put differently, ethics, like politics, is not a founded discipline, and hence it does not lend itself to scientistic philosophizing. It is initially merely a word, never definable in advance, that refers to the situatedness of man and the need to work out some provisional understandings on how to live collectively. It is therefore so much like politics that Aristotle and Plato could conceive the one to be the continuation of the other.

Gadamer's ethical thinking in his habilitation thesis is similarly conceived. It is first of all not a piece of moral philosophy and hence not the work of an academic "professional" philosopher. That is to say, Gadamer nowhere claims that there are founded and therefore privileged moral truths originating in the Bible, nature, reason, or even language from which one might deduce a moral system that could serve as a systematic guideline for politics. He thus has no "perfectionist ethics." On the contrary, he argues right from the outset a disavowal: ". . . not that Plato's ethics are dialectical but rather that dialectics are ethical. . . ." This would seem to be arguing a rationality principle, and it is if we are talking about the kind of discourse rationality I tried to sketch in at the outset of this book. But in any case, Gadamer's words are not setting forth a claim for a founded or substantive rationality. They are rather laying the groundwork for an ethics of responsibility by claiming that there is no privileged knowledge and that argumentation itself is the starting point for any responsible consideration of ethics.

The curious consequence of this is that there is apparently no discussion of ethics as such in Gadamer's habilitation thesis. Of course, this is a deception, for the entire habilitation thesis is one long discourse on ethics. It is more accurate, therefore, to say that there is no moral philosophizing in Gadamer's habilitation thesis. But with the claim that dialectics itself is ethical, if follows that all discussion of the structure of dialectical argumentation is also a discussion of how to lead the ethical life. Hence the habilitation thesis can be read not simply from the point of view of its contribution to language philosophy but also for its contribution to ethical thinking. But we must never forget that the discussion here is focused on discourse (or unfounded) rationality rather than substantive rationality.

Following the classical model, Max Weber made his argument on behalf of an ethics of responsibility in the context of an essay about politics. That is to say, where a perfectionist ethics might be appropriate to a religious association concerned about life in another world, an ethics of responsibility is the only ethics appropriate to this-worldly societies. Weber, adhering to Aristotle's mode of seeing ethics as the microcosm of the macrocosm of politics, was obviously reasoning backwards. He was, as his title indicates, discussing politics, and at the point where ethics came up was simply and consistently arguing that the laws of the political macrocosm were also applicable to the ethical microcosm. If responsibility is the chief rule of politics, then logically it ought to be the chief rule of ethics as well.

Gadamer proceeds in the reverse order. His introductory characterization of ethics as having no privileged truths virtually compels him to make some kind of statement about the political macrocosm. If ethics has no privileged truths, no doctrine of ideas, then logically it follows that the macrocosm of politics will also not have privileged truths to guide it. Gadamer's acceptance of the authenticity of the *Seventh Letter* and his construction of its meaning follow logically from his treatment of ethics in nonperfectionist terms. Thus does Gadamer adumbrate his discussion of the state in his habilitation thesis. The Gadamerian state is a very small Republic of Letters made up of Socrates and his Other, and eventually—after Socrates internalizes even this small community of two—the macrocosm of the state can be extrapolated from the microcosm of this critically thinking individual: the complete Platonic Socrates.[3]

II

These general insights into the character of Platonic ethics were given concrete shape by the early Gadamer in an unpublished paper written in 1930 and called *Practisches Wissen*, or "Practical Knowledge."[4] Perhaps more than any other writing of Gadamer's early period, it incorporated thoughts taken from Martin Heidegger, specifically from his 1923 seminar on Aristotle's *Nicomachean Ethics*. Yet even here, as I will show, Gadamer did not abandon the basic categories of thinking which he had taken from the Stefan George Circle. He rather incorporated Heidegger's insights into them and thereby achieved an outcome consistent with the direction of his own thought.

The problem of the paper was how we moderns with our Judeo-Christian concepts of ethics can ever come to understand classical Greek ethics.[5] In other words, how can we overcome our modern prejudice and thereby take the first step toward understanding a fundamentally different world. This is a problem not unlike the problem posed by Peter Winch in his piece called "Understanding a Primitive Society," except that here the other society is hardly "primitive" in the modern sense of the term.[6] Formulated more specifically, the problem is how anyone equipped with an "otherworldly" concept of ethics that emerges out of a religious way-of-life can grasp a "worldly" concept of ethics that emerges out of a political way-of-life.

Gadamer makes his problem more manageable by restating it as a distinctly philosophical question. Insofar as philosophy is a discipline, it operates through conceptualization and with the outcomes of this operation, namely, concepts. Philosophy distinguishes itself from other disciplines by being concerned with concepts that are universals, and insofar as it begins with wonder, it is wonder over these universals. These are the *logoi kath' auto* of Aristotle, and insofar as it is Aristotle who originated this particular intellectual activity, he is the originator of philosophy as we know it. Indeed, it is he who originated the problem of this unpublished and still untranslated 1930 paper, for the Judeo-Christian conception of morality as a relationship between otherworldly ideas of the good and worldly immorality first received its philosophical rendering, actually preconception, in Aristotle's thinking.

By arguing this way, Gadamer makes Aristotle into something of *bête noire*, but Gadamer does not trivialize the problem by personalizing it. That is to say, it is not claimed that Aristotle made his key move out of reasons of jealousy or stupidity. He did what he did because of a certain logic internal to philosophy. It was Aristotle, according to Gadamer, who first raised ethics "from the dialectical paradoxes of the Socratic question to the analytical clarity of the concept."[7] In his most dramatic formulation, Gadamer puts the matter as follows:

> The fate of philosophy first became visible in its world-historical form in Aristotle: the form of life, which it [Aristotelian philosophy] first painted with the grey on gray of concepts, was already old and could be recognized but not restored to its youth. In this manner,

Aristotle and the origin of the history of philosophy distinguished itself from the dialogical dialectic of Plato.[8]

We do well to underscore the significance of Gadamer's
characterization of philosophy at its origin. Philosophy is a
matter of conceptualization, of rendering life in the gray-on-
gray of precisely formulated concepts. Life, not life itself but
life as thought by a prephilosophical mind, is a three-dimensional *Gestalt*, a form in which elements are not separated out
by the analytical mind of the philosopher but are retained in
pictoral or narrative form.[9] The operation called "conceptualization" was what distinguished philosophy from life so formulated. But what distinguished philosophy from other possible
intellectual disciplines was its tendency toward universals, toward a concept of knowledge that was not local. It was this
possibility that Aristotle realized. In Gadamer's words:

> When Aristotle dissolved the connection between poli-
> tics and philosophy, it was not because he had recog-
> nized the untenability of a mathematical-universal
> grounding of politics but rather the other way round. It
> was because he realized the possibility of dissolving the
> philosophical universality of what is known from the
> life of the individual soul. Because concepts exist which
> determine what is meant and make it repeatable for
> everyone [the *logos kath' auto*], a philosophy equipped
> with this theoretical possibility will necessarily dis-
> solve its connection to politics.[10]

The issue in this paragraph can be formulated as a question
about truth. Philosophy emerged as a discipline independent
of politics because it realized the possibility of conceiving
truth-as-such, or universal truths. Politics, as a local affair, is
by nature only equipped with a capacity for realizing *truths-
for-us*, or local truths. Such a mode of doing philosophy paves
the way for the reception of Judeo-Christianity in the Western
mind. It undermines the more tribal instinct that tells us that

truth is something that applies in this valley but not the next, among the Azandi of East Africa but not among the English to the north, in Athens but not in Sparta.

When Gadamer goes on to say that this Aristotelian way of doing philosophy is for us virtually self-evident in its validity, he is only saying that we as moderns have come to grasp life as something that can be thought not just after it is lived but even before it is lived. This is the immanent possibility of universals: They are true not only at all places but also at all times. Morality, or the way we ought to live life, can be painted in the gray-on-gray of concepts before we live it. This is so taken for granted by us as moderns as to negate the necessity of argumentation. What is not so obvious is the Platonic indifference to this Aristotelian formulation of philosophy and its relation to life. It is at this point that Gadamer introduces his explanation of the unique quality of Platonic thinking:

> Plato does not address politics in terms of the principles of a theory of ideas, just as he does not instruct in terms of a doctrine of ideas. The high road to a vision of the high-heavenly scene and the low road of the self-concerned care [*Sorge*] for one's own being are one and the same way. Philosophy is not politics because Plato believed in a naive-abstract synthesis of the Good in the universe and the human world but rather because the philosopher and the statesman live in the same concern [*Sorge*]. Both must have true knowledge, and this means that they must know the Good. Yet one cannot know the Good from a detached and universal point of view but must rather know it originally for one's self. Only from this attending to one's own self (the soul) can true knowledge awake and bear fruits that are true. This caring is philosophy.[11]

It is well to pause at this point and reflect for a moment on what Gadamer, through Plato, is saying. He, as a budding professional philosopher, is not denying the possibility of universals. There is *truth-as-such* as well as *truth-for-us*. What Gadamer in this interpretation of Plato is doing is saving politics. In order to begin the climb up the ladder to *truth-as-such*, we must begin with the *truth-for-us* of politics. This negates the supposed classical distinction between *idea* and *doxa* as the thought materials, respectively, of philosophy and politics. It saves opinion as a form of local truth. It paves the way for an introduction of the Gadamerian notion of *prejudice* and, although Gadamer writing in 1930 did not yet have this handy concept, he did have a related word:

> The capacity to correctly judge the unique and to find the right way obviously grows with and out of life-experience. This means, however, out of a rising pre-knowledge [*Vorwissen*]. Nonetheless, the authentic essence of *phronesis* exists in this capacity for on-the-spot thinking, and the substantive pre-knowledge which accompanies concrete reflection is secondary. (An increase of this pre-knowledge, as is the case with an 'ethic', is only an increase of concrete, practical consciousness. . . .)[12]

The point of introducing the notion of *vorwissen*, or "pre-knowledge," was to support the claim that that practical knowledge has a historical dimension. Yet the formulation here is nearly poetic, and it is not yet as rigorous as Gadamer would make it. It thus behooves us to go on to another argument which is more rigorous in the way it addresses the question of the different forms of knowledge.

III

Gadamer began his paper with a defense of the Platonic Socrates against the charge of intellectualism, and it is by this means that the problem of knowledge was introduced. The claim that Socrates reduced ethics to knowledge is for Gadamer not merely absurd but also deeply revealing about the modern mind and its prejudices. For implicit in the claim of intellectualism is the prejudiced view that knowledge and action are two entirely different things. If knowledge is the acquisition of *truth-as-such*, then the charge of intellectualism makes sense. But if knowledge is a local affair, a matter of *truth-for-us*, then the charge of intellectualism makes no sense at all, for action is also a local affair and as such cannot be separated from local knowledge. From this point of view, the modern claim of intellectualism reflects more on the questioner than on Socrates. In Gadamer's words:

> To test surrounding truths in terms of their reality and their effectiveness was not the introduction of something new. It was rather a matter of taking old truths seriously, of taking them as if they were what they wanted to be. This was the sense of Socratic dialogue. It had its peculiar power in the demonstration of ignorance, because for it the connection between knowledge and reality was indissoluble. That which is called *knowledge* in this Socratic equation must therefore emerge from the mandatory connection of reality and *prāxis*. To presuppose knowledge in which this equation is incomprehensible or forced in effect turns the charge of intellectualism against one's self.[13]

Not only is the charge of intellectualism against the Platonic Socrates absurd. Equally absurd is the claim that Socrates was motivated by an interest in pure, mindless action. This takes the form of a claim that Socrates was the first utilitarian.[14] Against this charge, Gadamer defends the Platonic Socrates in detail, and while it will be worth our while to recount Gadamer's argument, it is also helpful to set it in context, and this means dealing with the subject matter of Heidegger's 1923 seminar on Aristotle's *Nicomachean Ethics*.

Book Six of the *Nicomachean Ethics* deals with knowledge and attempts to establish its different forms.[15] However incomplete the discussion is, it demonstrates that philosophy at its birth was capable of self-reflection, by which I mean reflection on the various modes by which the mind was capable of thinking and gaining knowledge. Aristotle discussed several different modes, the chief among which being *episteme*, or exact knowledge, *techne*, or applied knowledge, and *phronesis*, or knowledge of how to get along in the intersubjective human world. It is helpful to give a thumbnail sketch of these forms before turning to Gadamer.

The natural sciences as we know them aim at exact knowledge, or *episteme*. They thus produce theories that are submitted to the test of logical coherence as well as correspondence to reality. Darwin's theory of natural selection or Einstein's theory of relativity are *epistemes* insofar as they are logically coherent and compelling as well as accurate in their correspondence to reality. They are, however, macrotheoretical theories insofar as they fit only a reality larger than that accessible to the human senses. At the less arcane level of a life lived in Chicopee, Massachusetts, a theory of social selection might work better than the theory of natural selection to explain mating patterns. Similarly, on the planet earth, the theories of Newtonian physics are still much more applicable than Einstein's theory of relativity.

My point is that exact knowledge is not always practical. Therefore we have *techne*, or applied scientific knowledge. The construction of a motor, for example, is an activity understandable as applied science. Yet a motor, for example an automobile engine, is not a simple application of scientific principles. There is no way that a motor can be constructed in terms of any single, logically coherent scientific theory. It is rather a combination of theories of mechanics, electronics, hydraulics, thermodynamics, and the like. Put differently, one can analyze a successful automobile engine in terms of exact scientific theories, but never in terms of one exact scientific theory.

What this suggests is that *techne* is a form of knowledge separate from the exact natural sciences. It is a matter of applying
the otherworldly knowledge of the exact sciences to the de-
manding natural confines of the human condition.

The most basic organizational categories of German universities are the *Naturwissenschaften* and the *Geisteswissenschaften*. They may be said to correspond to the two principles
of knowledge spelled out above. The natural sciences, including mathematics, aim at exact knowledge, and in doing so
they serve industry, which aims at the technical application of
exact theoretical knowledge. But what about the *Geisteswissenschaften*? Do the human sciences aim at understanding human cultural achievements as an application of the principles
of exact knowledge? The hidden premise here is that the universe is a logically coherent place that can be fully understood
in terms of universal principles and their local application.
Arguably, this is the way Marx understood history. When he
said that culture was epiphenomenal, he meant that it was determined by the forces and relations of production, and he saw
these are determined by exact principles of nature, understandable by the natural sciences. Hobbes and Saint-Simon
before him and Marx, Lenin, and Taylor after him are not all
that different from Marx. They see the *Geisteswissenschaften*
as a local application of the principles discovered in the *Naturwissenschaften*. Contemporary German academics, especially
those in the institutes built around *Neuphilologie*, would not
like the above formulation, but they are not always philosophically equipped to argue against it.

Contemporary German scholars would rightly object that
the organization of knowledge in German universities was
and is more complicated than is indicated above. But in order
to philosophically argue their case, they would have to propose
a different concept of knowledge, and this might lead them to
a rediscovery of Aristotle. As already noted, he conceived a
third category of knowledge, namely, *phronesis*. This was a
kind of knowledge that was necessary for getting along with

and among other human beings. Yet even though Aristotle discussed *phronesis* as a concept, it is by no means certain that we can grasp and use this concept of knowledge.

It can be understood, although by no means explained, by reference to the basic organizational structure of American universities. In contrast to the twofold German division into the *Naturwissenschaften* and the *Geisteswissenschaften*, we divide up our academic pie into the natural sciences, the social sciences, and the humanities. We understand the first in terms of the ideal type called *episteme*, or the quest for exact knowledge. We are less clear about the social sciences, but if the current status of the field of economics is any indication, the social sciences aim at becoming a kind of technical science, a field in which the exact knowledge of the natural sciences is blended into a smoothly functioning motor.

We Americans generally stand somewhat perplexed when confronting the humanities, however. We cannot explain and justify them in terms of *episteme* or *techne*. Like our German colleagues, we usually do not have a concept of knowledge to provide a rigorous philosophical defense of their continued existence. It does not follow from this that we are silenced, however, for this scandal causes no end of debate. At the everyday level of college curriculum committees in American colleges and universities, the humanities survive because most academics are simply too embarrassed to vote against them or because of the appealing argument that they help scientists and social engineers to succeed in life. They provide the 'finish' that distinguishes the so-called educated man from the masses of technocrats. These of course are hardly philosophical justifications. They are practical, sociological justifications, and while not reducible to *techne* for their justification, they lack a concept of knowledge that might stabilize their existence.

If we look to the more arcane level of contemporary philosophizing, we find much the same situation. Richard Rorty's *Philosophy and the Mirror of Nature*, for example, rightly argues that philosophy should not be conducted according to the canons of *episteme*, but when it comes to providing a justification for the kind of philosophy Rorty wants, he is only able to spin out large sections about "endless conversations" and the like. What can be said of Rorty can also, I believe, be said of Bernstein, Oakeshott, or Habermas. They all argue well enough against "scientism" in human affairs, but they do not argue nearly well enough for an alternative which justifies our belief in the humanities as a distinct form of knowledge that exists by virtue of something more than the suffrage of so-called *educated persons*.

This genuinely scandalous state of affairs does not characterize Aristotle's thinking. He introduces a term, *phronesis*, and places it alongside *episteme* and *techne* as a form of knowledge. He thus provides the philosophical justification for what in American universities are called the "humanities," and he sets the stage for a challenge to the domination of scientism (*techne*) in the social sciences. Unfortunately, he does not adequately spell out what practical knowledge is, and hence book six of the *Nicomachean Ethics* leaves us with a problem that has long perplexed philosophers. It also provides Gadamer with his starting point in the unpublished paper called *"Pracktisches Wissen."* Now, with this as background, precisely what is it that Gadamer has to say about *phronesis*?

First, the form of knowledge called *phronesis* is characterized by Gadamer as being existential.[16] It comes into being when we grasp that technical knowledge cannot answer the question of how we are to exist. Technical knowledge, rightly understood, is prior knowledge of how to do something. By being prior, it allows us to distance ourselves from human situations. But existence, as Gadamer understands it, is revealed at precisely the point when it presents us with *situations* for which no advance knowledge is appropriate. In a workshop, we always know what to do with tools. But then one day our hammer breaks. De we know how to "help ourselves" is such a situation. At such a point, the mystique of *techne* is broken and an existential crisis, admittedly poetic, is introduced. Gadamer does not use this illustration from Heidegger, but this is what he means.

Second, there is an excellence (*arete*) to technical knowledge that is now a part of practical knowledge.[17] One can get better at using a tool by practicing with it. But the maxim that "practice makes perfect" does not apply to existential situations. One cannot get better at handling unique situations, and it is precisely this uniqueness and newness that distinguishes the existential from the routine. To the extent that family crises are routine, the police can learn to manage them by means of simulations, but to the extent that a situation is really unique, there is no excellence that can be gained by practicing how to handle it. *Phronesis* therefore has a somewhat messy quality to it, and as such it shows itself to be the virtue or form of knowledge best keyed to existence defined as situatedness.

Third, as has already been pointed out above, practical knowledge is not fully without history. One cannot step outside existence and practice for it, but one can accumulate life experience and thus gain a sense of how to act in a unique situation. But this prior knowledge (*Vorwissen*) is really a kind of "prejudice," for the simple reason that there is no final guarantee that it will work. Technical knowledge, viewed as advance knowledge, is not really "prejudice" because it is guaranteed by the exactness of scientific knowledge. It really does yield predictive power. But not so practical knowledge. In its accumulated, historical form, it is always, at best, approximate, and that is why it is a matter of "prejudice." If it were anything other than that, then it would deny the surprising, really new quality of existence. With this argument Gadamer provides a rationale for his concept of prejudice.

Fourth, there is a curious lack of free choice to *phronesis* which is not a part of technical knowledge.[18] We can always choose our professions, and when we choose one, this means that we choose not to practice the others. We can then practice our trades on a nine-to-five basis, so to speak. Or we cannot practice with our tools, and consequently we can forget the skills we have acquired. None of this is true of practical knowledge. We cannot freely choose not to exist. No matter what our chosen profession, we will be confronted every day with existential situations that call upon practical knowledge. We can try to reduce the scope of practical knowledge by applying technical knowledge, but we are unlikely to succeed. We cannot forget our own existence. We can pretend to, but it will haunt us, and so we do better to confront it.

Fifth and finally, where technical knowledge is for the most part in the service of the body, practical knowledge is in the service of the human soul, and what is good for the body is not necessarily good for the soul.[19] Because the soul is not the body, the question of the Idea of the Good is raised as a philosophical problem. Gadamer does not treat it exhaustively in this early paper, but he does say enough to indicate the direction of his thought.

I have already said something about this above, so here it is entirely possible to settle for a summary overview. For Plato, according to Gadamer, the Idea of the Good is not divisible. It functions at the micro level of the individual and at the macro level of the larger signboard of the *polis* and even at a cosmic level. The key point to make with Plato is that there is no high road and low road to the vision of the Good, that is to say, no distinction between philosophy and politics. The same, however, cannot be said of Aristotle. Because of the possibility presented by the notion of a universal truth (*logos kath' auto*), Aristotle was able to make a separation and speak of a Good-as-such and a Good-for-us (or a Good-for-me). In other words, Aristotle was able to separate philosophy as the pursuit of the Idea of the Good-as-such from politics as the pursuit of the Idea of the Good-for-us. It is with this separation that Gadamer disagrees.

Hence Gadamer can finally speak of a "political *phronesis*" and mean by this a sense of how human relations are organized in the spheres of economics, government, legislation, and justice.[20] Statesmen, such as Pericles, can be characterized as *phronomoi* and recognized by thinkers such as Aristotle as being distinct from philosophers because what they do is based on a different concept of knowledge. Indeed, Aristotle is still well enough attuned to the real meaning of *phronesis* to

be capable of distinguishing political scientists from statesmen. The early version of the political scientist is to be found
in those "stateless statesmen, the sophists, who teach the art
of governing from books as if it were a *techne*."[21]

IV

The unpublished 1930 paper called *"Practisches Wissen"* incorporates much of what transpired in Heidegger's 1923 seminar on Aristotle's *Nicomachean Ethics*. Clearly, however, it is
not dominated by Heidegger. It is rather framed in terms of
categories provided by the Stefan George Circle and hence
dovetails nicely with what Gadamer had already done in his
habilitation thesis. This can be seen in the large role assigned
to the figure of Socrates in this paper, but more clearly it can
be seen in Gadamer's final paragraph, where he uses the Georgian term *Gestalt* several times to describe the problem he is
trying to come to grips with.

I would hazard the guess that Gadamer early realized that
Heidegger's thinking was itself a conceptualization of existen-
tialism. In this respect, the virtue of the thinking of the Stefan
George Circle was to be found in its refusal to conceptualize
existence. Precisely this characteristic, of course, forced the
Georgians to the margin of the German academic world or
beyond. But simultaneously it was this revived three-dimensional thinking that enabled Georgians like Hildebrandt or
Friedemann to *save* Plato and the Platonic Socrates from the
rejection they had undergone at the hands of Nietzsche and,
later, Heidegger.

The gray-on-gray of Aristotelian conceptualization could
not really capture the three-dimensional liveliness of Greek
ethics. It could only remind us of what had once been alive but
was now flattened out into concepts. If one persists and asks
what it was that was sought by Greek ethics, Gadamer's an-

swer—formulated at the end of this essay—was that it was a *menschlicher Gestalt*, a human form. This is, according to Gadamer, the beautiful, and it is in the realization of *der schönen Gestalt*, the beautiful form, that practical knowledge took shape. That this was the life of Socrates is clear from the opening pages of Gadamer's paper, where Socrates is defended against the charge of intellectualism with the argument that it was he and practically he alone who understood that the Idea of the Good could not be separated from everyday political life. Gadamer's paper is not so much a rejection of Aristotelian *concept* philosophy as a necessary corrective to it. My point is to recognize that this corrective was only made possible by Gadamer's early association with the Georgians and the philological tradition they represented. It is hardly accidental that the final words of Gadamer's unpublished 1930 paper bring us back to "the dialogical dialectics of Plato."[22]

6

Poets, Education,
and
the State

I

All that has been said about ethics in the two previous chapters is said by way of preparation for Gadamer's more focused discussion of the state in two essays written in the 1930s. The first is a discussion of the peculiar problem of Plato's relation with the poets of Athens, contained in Gadamer's long paper entitled "Plato and the Poets."[1] This problem is usually handled under the academic category of Plato's *philosophy of art*, but my claim here will be that Gadamer's essay makes much more sense if its focus is taken to be *philosophy of politics*. That is to say, the immediate problem between Plato and the poets obviously is an issue of the artful use of language, but this issue can be best understood if it is grasped in terms of its consequences to ethics and politics.

The fact that Gadamer introduces his concept of *aesthetic consciousness* in "Plato and the Poets" does not jeopardize the claim that the main thread of "Plato and the Poets" is one of political theorizing.[2] Plato is not criticized by Gadamer in the usual modern fashion for his failure to appreciate art. It is rather the other way around: Abstracted art is being criticized by Gadamer's Plato for its failure to appreciate the irreducibly ethical dimension of the *polis*. The language of the poets has to be expelled so that true dialogue can be restored. Hence Gadamer's thinking in "Plato and the Poets," with its main thread in politics, is fully and rigorously consistent with his thinking in his first article on Werner Jaeger and with his habilitation thesis: Politics, as the continuation of ethics by other means, is governed by the same norms as ethics.

Similarly, the brief essay called "Plato's Educational State" can easily be misunderstood if we treat it out of context and fail to credit the mind of the early Gadamer with its characteristic persistence and consistency.[3] Here, too, Gadamer is not being an academic philosopher interested in Plato's *philosophy of education*. Just as art is not the main thread of "Plato and the Poets," so too education is not the main thread of "Plato's Educational State." Education is understood and judged by Gadamer according to what it contributes to the formation of the human soul, and the reason for wanting a soul (if we have to ask) is because we are ethical beings. Put somewhat differently, it is because we have so little (instinctual) inscribed or, better, *written* nature to guide our actions that it is our (civilized) nature to need a soul, or a harmonious makeup, as prelude to decision in the world of action. It is the state's chief function to shape that soul.

Hence, finally, with "Plato's Educational State," we return to the theme which has been given so much emphasis in this book: the idea of *Gestalt*. I argued that in his habilitation thesis Gadamer was inclined to write a biography of Socrates along the model of the genre established in the Stefan George Circle. But because Gadamer was a good deal cleverer than most members of the Stefan George Circle, he took this mandate figuratively rather than literally. Therefore, the *Gestalt* of the Platonic Socrates turns out to be an exercise in bringing into high relief the elements of a speaking civilization: dialogue and dialectic. We do well to understand that this occurs because the Platonic Socrates, Gadamer's Platonic Socrates, is emphatically an ethical being. If Plato's ethics is dialectical, as Gadamer claims, then the Platonic Socrates—as a thoroughly ethical being—ought to be given over equally thoroughly to dialogue and dialectics. How else can he lead the ethical life?

The function of "Plato's Educational State" can also be understood—indeed, it can only be understood—in terms of the necessity of giving a *Gestalt* to the human soul. Hence what begins with an effort to portray the *Gestalt* of a single individual ends with the effort to portray the *Gestalt* of the entire community. There is thus a common ethical thread running through Gadamer's early writings from beginning to end, but unfortunately it is difficult to see because of the sheer quantitative imbalance of Gadamer's early writings. The theme of Plato's relation to the poets is a detail in Plato's intellectual biography, and frankly it deserves no more attention than Gadamer gave it. But the theme of Plato's educational state is no such minor detail. As Gadamer's emphasis on the authenticity of the *Seventh Letter* tells us, there is nothing more important in Plato interpretation than the recognition that politics provides Plato's classical thinking with its point of departure.

Hence, I would argue, Gadamer's early period should have ended with a book entitled *Plato's Educational State*. It did not. It rather ended with a short article with the same title, and Gadamer then never again came back to this thread. I will thus have to give Gadamer's last early writing short shrift but want to note here that the failure to write a *Gestalt*-biography of the Platonic state is the single most significant failing of the early period of Gadamer's career. Indeed, it is this failing that puts an end to Gadamer's early period, and it is probably the main reason why so little attention has been paid to his early writings.

II

Language and education do not proceed in a vacuum but rather are always already situated or contextualized in the *polis*, and the *polis* is constituted as a set of unwritten laws by which persons relate to each other in society.[4] Gadamer's grasp of the *polis* in "Plato and the Poets" is subtle and compelling. He pays no attention to the tip of the political iceberg formed by written laws or visible forms of government, the characteristic concern of *Altertumswissenschaft*. He is much more concerned for the unwritten laws of society and the unformed government of persons who take advantage of those unwritten laws. In classical Athens, according to Gadamer, "the ethos prevailing in . . . society which, though concealed, secretly molds human beings" is articulated by the poets, who therefore act as a kind of unformulated government of the state.[5] Plato's struggle with the poets is not, as Nietzsche would have us believe, an artistic contest. It is rather a political struggle for the government of Athens.

The poets, in effect, are authorized to give *Gestalt* to the unseen *polis*, and this *polis* is in turn authorized to give *Gestalt* to the souls of the young men of Athens. The issue in "Plato and the Poets" appears to be language, and indeed this is the stated issue, but the specific language of the poets is brought to issue because of what it contributes to the *Gestaltung* or formation of the Athenian *polis* and the soul of every Athenian. And to the extent that Plato has an alternative to the language of the poets, it is because he better understands the problems of *Gestaltung*. It is therefore that Gadamer's Plato once again opts for dialogue and dialectics, for the spoken language over the written language. The soul of Athens and its citizens is the real underlying issue.

By the late fifth century, what Gadamer calls a "binding political ethos" had ceased to exist in Athens, and I take Gadamer to mean by this that the Athenians had lost their self-conscious relation to public ethics.[6] By this Gadamer did not mean that ethics had been privatized. Rather, what came to exist was a situation in which unwritten political rules of private aggrandizement had replaced the unwritten rules of a more community-oriented ethics. In sum, *Gesellschaft* had replaced *Gemeinschaft*. It was in this situation that the real class of conspirators, the Sophists, were able to rise to prominence as a class of educators. They simply made explicit and politically operative what was already implicit in the existing Greek *polis*. "For the sophists," Gadamer notes, "ethical principles are no longer valid in themselves but only as a form of our mutual 'keeping an eye' on one another."[7] The basic unwritten rule of the Athenian constitution, according to Gadamer, is the following: *No one does what is right voluntarily.*[8] The unwritten ethics of Greece are such as to record the destruction of the public sphere of Greek life.

The question that arose for Plato, according to Gadamer, was whether to reform the existing state or go beyond it in a quest for a much more radical solution. Plato's choice was against reform, and hence in favor of philosophy conceived as a more radical solution to political problems. This being the case, the quarrel with the poets was radically political. In brief, the basic problem was with the poets's use of language to shape the psyche. The quarrel with the poets was in no manner a simple quarrel over aesthetics. In Gadamer's words, the

> . . . actual truth of the matter is that the meaning and intent of [Plato's] critique of the poets can be established only by departing from the place where it occurs. It is found in Plato's work on the state [the *Republic*] . . . which is erected before our eyes in words alone from the building blocks which alone suffice for it. The critique of the poets can be understood only within the setting of this total refounding of a new state in words of philosophy, only understood as a radical turning away from the existing state.[9]

What we need to note here is the combination of approaches associated above with the influence of the poet Stefan George and his Circle and that of the new way of doing philosophy of Martin Heidegger. The Platonic idea of the state, for example, is one in which language obviously does not express something outside it. Language is rather thoroughly creative. Creativity now refers to ethical rules, and the idea or claim being put forth is that the state creates ethical rules without any prior determination from outside. In other words, public dialogue itself is ethical because it is the rational procedure by which ethical rules are arrived at.

Indeed, to take this idea one step further, the Platonic state is itself a creation in words. Gadamer says as much several times in his 1934 essay: Plato's state is "a state which is erected before our eyes in words alone from the building blocks which alone suffice for it."[10] Or elsewhere: "For that reason [to awaken the powers which form the state] Socrates erects a state in words, the possibility of which is given only in *philosophy*."[11] The Platonic state is, Gadamer tells us, "a state in thought, not any state on earth." And as with any state in words, its purpose is "to bring something to light and not to provide an actual design for an improved order in real political life."[12] It is a pure creation of the well-tuned soul, that of the Platonic Socrates, and it is undertaken because of the felt need of the well-tuned soul to exist in a supportive context. It is a paradigm "for someone who wants to order *himself* and his own inner constitution. Its sole raison d'être is to make it possible for a person to recognize himself in the paradigm. Of course the point is precisely that he who recognizes himself therein does not recognize himself as an isolated individual without a state."[13] Platonic philosophy can therefore not be grasped if that philosophy is treated as an expression of something outside it. Quite literally, it has to be taken on its own terms. Plato's philosophy of art is therefore a detail that will be hermeneutically interpreted by being referred back to this political context. This approach, to use Gadamer's words, is *total*, it is the *actual truth*, and it gets at the *intent* of Plato's philosophy.

Now at this point we should pause to be clear as to what the political context is that is being referred to here. Once again, it is not any context that is outside Plato's writings. That is to say, Plato is not a *Realist* in the Aristotelian sense of the term. Gadamer makes this clear in his essay. He says at a key point in his argument that Platonic justice "is no longer to be clearly identified with any given *reality* [my italics]."[14] What then is it to be identified with? In Gadamer's words, "when knowledge of it must be defended against the arguments of a new 'enlightened' consciousness, a *philosophical conversation* about the true state becomes the only true praise of justice."[15] Hence if we want to know what the phrases "the state in words" or "the city in speech" refer to, the answer is that they describe a philosophical conversation, such as the one Gadamer wrote about in his habilitation thesis. If, as Gadamer claimed in 1928, dialectics is ethical, then we can already make the guess that dialectics is also political. In 1934 Gadamer finally says as much.

The context of Plato's ethics is politics, then, but the politics are ideal, not real. This is not to say that so-called political reality does not play a role in shaping Plato's political thinking. In fact, as we shall soon find out, it plays a decisive negative role. Political reality, in the commonsense use of that term, is precisely what Plato wants to change. Yet once Plato has made his case against political reality, he has to go on and make a positive case for the ideal city, and this is the city in speech.

The problem with the poets, according to Gadamer, is that they *imitate* rather than create. Put differently, the poets use words to express a reality outside their language. Gadamer then argues why this is a problem: "He who really imitates and only imitates, in mime, is no longer himself. He gives himself an alien character."[16] Without ever using the Heideggerian term, the entire argument is then keyed to the issue of human authenticity. The term Gadamer does use is *self*, and it occurs repeatedly in his argument: Imitation produces a "split in the self;" it induces a "turning away from oneself." The person engaging in it becomes "oblivious to himself," he does not "preserve himself." Imitation leads to "self-exteriorization," or to "self-estrangement," or to "self-alienation," or to "self-forgetting." So here Gadamer is employing that key theme of German nineteenth-century thought: The purpose of education is to construct an authentic human being, and this has to be done in terms of an image of the *self*.[17] The purpose of poetry is to provide an image of all that human beings can be, and at least in the classical age of Greece poetry was failing to do this.

Plato's critique of imitation "is at the same time a *critique of the moral problematic of AESTHETIC CONSCIOUSNESS.*"[18] This is Gadamer's italicization and capitalization, and hence it seems fair to infer that he intends to emphasize the destructiveness of this form of consciousness. In grasping fully what the term means in this essay, we can do no better than to turn back to the lengthy paragraph with the recurrent references to the self. The really operative German word that describes what happens to the self in a society dominated by poets is *äussern*. Christopher Smith translates this term as "exteriorize" or "external," or the like. He is not mistaken, but the German term can also be correctly translated as *express*, thereby recapturing the thread originating in the Stefan George Circle's thinking. Thus a person who is characterized by an aesthetic consciousness is one who is expressing values that are inauthentic. He is what Heidegger would have called a mass man. Along similar lines, art or literature that imitates is expressing something outside itself, and this makes it inauthentic.

Political reality in classical Athens was inauthentic in this way. Poets did not take themselves to be creative beings. They rather believed that they were expressing Homer, or to put this in Gadamer's terms, "the role of the poets in Greek education [was] to justify the whole of one's knowledge—in any area—by recourse to Homer."[19] Their knowledge was thus inauthentic because it was imitative, or expressive of something outside their own poetry. In the listeners (readers) to the poetry, this had the effect of corrupting them by making them forget themselves: "Aesthetic self-forgetfulness afforded to the sophistry of the passions an entree into the human heart."[20] This microcosmic relationship then grew and took community-wide form. Classical politics, according to Gadamer, then took on the "colors of the Athenian theatrocracy."[21]

The term *aesthetic consciousness* can be given added understanding by referring it back to the German nineteenth century. The original purpose of subjecting Germans to the study of classical Greece was to provide them with a model which would bring out the fullest humanity in modern Germans. Nietzsche was the first to recognize that *Altertumswissenschaft* had defeated this purpose by presenting a Greece that was all factual and hence easily imitated. Nietzsche reintroduced a countervailing and counter-factual notion of Greece, placing heavy emphasis on the irrational in the *Birth of Tragedy*. Nietzsche was not interested in the irrational for its own sake but rather for what it revealed to us about the creative. Unquestionably Nietzsche exaggerated, but he nonetheless launched a mode of interpreting Greece that led directly to Rohde's *Psyche* and to Freudian psychology. The Greeks—Nietzsche's Greeks—were not to be imitated at all. The thread that began with Nietzsche thus is one that intends to do battle with an *aesthetic consciousness* of the Greeks characteristic of the positivism of *Altertumswissenschaft*. Gadamer is here articulating that thread.

The reality of classical Greece is that the human psyche is alienated from itself. It has become other-directed, imitative, and hence uncreative. Plato intends to move away from this aestheticized reality toward the authenticity of ideality. But how? That is the next step, and with Gadamer it is not at all a logical step. That is to say, there is nothing in aestheticized reality that leads one to recognize it for what it is. It is a cave, and the way out of it is not at all logical.

Hence in the progress of Gadamer's argument, the next step is a *decision*, a completely original starting point that does not express anything outside itself. Gadamer says this more than once: when speaking of Plato, Gadamer notes that "his position is the quite conscious expression of a decision, a decision made as a result of having been taken with Socrates and philosophy."[22] This decision was "made in opposition to the entire political and intellectual culture of his time, and made in the conviction that philosophy alone has the capacity to save the state."[23] And elsewhere Gadamer criticizes the poet because the persons he cannot abide are those who "preserve that quiet energy which grows from resolve."[24] The emphasis is on an origin that comes from an authentic personality.

We should understand that the emerging hero of Gadamer's argument is none other than Plato himself. It is he, Plato, who has the resolve and the conviction to burn his poetry and make a fresh start on the project of politics. However briefly, the emerging figure of Plato is therefore similar to the *Gestalt* figures described in the biographies of the members of the Stefan George Circle. They were creators *ex nihilo*, writers who did not express some truth or reality outside their writings but who instead used words to create new reality. That is what Plato will now do when he creates a city in speech. He will demonstrate that politics at its ideal essence is the opposite of accepting the dictates of reality.

Yet there is nothing mysterious about the city in speech. No matter how Gadamer describes it, what we finally see is that Plato's language returns us, quite literally, to the soul. The ideal city is very much the opposite of the real city. Where the real city alienates the self, the ideal city returns the self to itself. But this ideal city is in language, so it behooves us to inquire into how this return is brought about.

III

The problem with the language of the poets is that it is imitative, and so we can expect the same arguments to be employed against it by Gadamer as were earlier aired in reference to human psychology. And sure enough, Gadamer, in following his Plato, does just this. He of course refers to the *Ion*, an early Platonic writing that records a conversation between Socrates and the rhapsode Ion. It is here that Plato attacks the poets for being inspired, by which he means that they are filled with the gods and hence do not express themselves. When Gadamer says that the poets are "less qualified to interpret than are any of their listeners" he means that they lack any authentic intention of their own that would enable them to understand why poetry exists and what can be done with it.[25] The poet is, once again quoting Plato, a winged and holy thing who cannot create until he is filled by the god and is "unconscious and reason is no longer in him."[26]

Gadamer notes that Plato is not the first classical Greek to criticize Homer's poetry. The great tragedians of the fifth century did this as well, but Gadamer argues that "Plato's criticism goes "infinitely further."[27] "Drama too falls before his critique," for the reason that it too is basically imitative.[28] Gadamer's point is that Plato does not simply want to take down Homer. He would have been in good and moderate company if that were his sole aim. Plato is actually much more radical than this. He wants to take down the entire poetic form of language, and the basic reason for this is that poetic language is irreducibly imitative.

Here as elsewhere, Gadamer is consistent with the language philosophy of the Stefan George Circle. Correctly understood, the problem for the Georgians was not so much that language was imitative or expressive of something outside it. Everyday language had always functioned this way, and no purpose was served in endless criticism of the prosaic quality of everyday life. The problem was rather that *Dichtung*, or poetry, was a peculiar form of language insofar as its authenticity depended upon it being self-sufficient. The more reasonable among the Georgians would always have recognized that prose expresses something outside it, but they wished to reserve a purity for *Dichtung* that would enable it to lay claim to being a creative source—and hence a *linguistic* foundation

—for human life. Thus the corruption of poetry in the nineteenth century was for the Georgians a serious matter. It had
to be combatted by restoring poetry to its pristine purity, and
this was a central mission of the Georgians. It is at this point
that Gadamer necessarily would break with the Georgians, for
his Plato was not intent on restoring poetry but rather in re-
placing Homeric poetry with prosaic, *but creative*, philosophic
language.

Poetry, whether it be that of Homer or that of Aeschylus,
was basically narrative, and so it was utterly dependent upon
direct speech. This quality of poetry could not have been reformed without fundamental changes in grammatical structure, and these were more the product of the slow development
of Greek culture than anything else. *Indirect speech* did not occur in archaic, tribal Greece. It was the consequence of gradual urbanization and the slowly dawning awareness that the
problems of living together, ethical problems, could be handled more gracefully by a language that offered the speaker
the possibility of distancing himself from the action. This
grammatical possibility was fully in place by the time Plato
lived, and hence Plato was able to write differently than Homer and approach the ethical problems of classical Greek society with a more appropriate because more nuanced language.
Gadamer rightly notes that Plato was fully conscious of this
possibility and hence demonstrated a language consciousness
that supposedly did not exist in classical Greece.[29] Gadamer
takes the following example from the *Iliad*:

> And as he wandered on, now alone, the old
> man
> Implored Apollo, the son of long-locked Letho,
> fervently.
> Hear me, oh god, who with silver bow dost
> bestride Chrysa
> And holy Cilla, thou who are the mighty lord
> of Tenedos.

Smintheus! If ever I have built a lovely temple
   for you
If even I have burnt for thee choice
   shanks
Of bulls or of goats, then grant me this,
   my desire:
May the Achaeans pay for my tears under
   thy shafts.[30]

Plato then rewrites this in the *Republic* as follows:

And the old man on hearing this was frightened and de-
parted in silence, and having gone apart from the camp
he prayed at length to Apollo, invoking the appellations
of the god, and reminding him of, and asking requital
for, any of his gifts that had found favor whether in the
building of temples or the sacrifice of victims. In return
for these things he prayed that the Achaeans should
suffer for his tears by the god's shafts.[31]

The argument in reference to these passages is primarily
philological but it has significance for the emergence of philosophy: Homer could not have written in indirect speech because
that grammatical form was a late development in the ancient
Greek language. Indeed Plato was one of the first Greek writers to use indirect speech extensively, and when Plato has the
Platonic Socrates announce his intent to use indirect speech, it
is by having Socrates claim that he is not a poetic man. [*Republic*, 394a]. Unlike Monsieur Jourdain, then, Socrates is not
just discovering that he has been speaking prose for forty
years without being aware of it. He is rather shifting from direct to indirect speech because this is a new possibility of the
ancient Greek language.

We must then ask why the Platonic Socrates would make
such a shift. One answer is readily apparent in the *Republic*.
Indirect speech has the distinct advantage of allowing the

emotions to be detached from the subject being discussed. Direct speech, in contrast, blends emotions and action into one literary form and thus makes literature a problem as well as a pleasure. Literature is a pleasure because we are able to feel what is happening but a problem because our own feelings as readers interfere with our thinking about what is happening. Indirect speech, because it is so much more devoid of immediate emotional content, facilitates thinking what we are doing. I am not saying that rendering an action in indirect speech is the same as thinking what we are doing but rather that it is the condition of the possibility of such thought.

Thus indirect speech is necessary to the emergence of philosophy insofar as philosophy is a matter of reasoned rather than impassioned argument. That Plato is aware of this is clear from many of his best writings. Socrates is always portrayed as someone who, whatever else his strengths and virtues, is in control of his emotions. His antagonists, in contrast, are not nearly so in control and are also, not surprisingly, inclined to use direct speech. Now I am not so much talking about poets as about sophists. For example, Thrasymachus comes on stage in the *Republic* in the following introduction:

> Now Thrasymachus had many times started out to take over the argument of our discussion, but had been restrained by the men sitting near him, who wanted to hear the argument out. But when we paused and I said this, he could no longer keep quiet; hunched up like a wild beast, he flung himself at us as if to tear us to pieces.[32]

But by the middle of the discussion, Thrasymachus has been cured of his emotionalism, his *language of action*, and this has been very much a matter of weaning him from direct speech and bringing him over to indirect speech:

> Now Thrasymachus did not agree to all of this so easily as I tell it now, but he dragged his feet and resisted,

and he produced a wonderful quantity of sweat, for it
was summer. And then I saw what I had not yet seen
before—Thasymachus blushing.[33]

By the end of the argument, Thrasymachus is a different man,
and the difference is in no small measure due to the kind of
speech used by Socrates. With tact that is the consequence of
his self-control, Socrates gives Thrasymachus credit for the resulting quality of argument:

> "I owe it to you, Thrasymachus," I said, "since you
> have gotten gentle and have left off being hard on
> me."[34]

Socrates has in effect gained a conversation partner, a significant Other. Although Gadamer does not handle these materials in this manner, everything he goes on to say about the
Platonic use of language points in this direction. For the key
to understanding language in Plato is the effect language has
in returning us to ourselves, more accurately, to an authentic
vision of the philosophic *self* in us. This is a self that is capable
of engaging in sustained discourse, undetermined by privileged knowledge claims, aimed at reaching agreement about
the meaning of a moral concept, and thereby capable of serving as a foundation for whatever community human beings
are capable of achieving.

I have taken the liberty of drawing this conclusion out of
Plato for the simple reason that it has been a direction pointed
at by Gadamer from his earliest writing on Werner Jaeger's
thinking and through his habilitation thesis. It is a direction
which continues in "Plato and the Poets," but often in more
suggestive than developed form. What was initially an emphasis on a speaking as opposed to a writing culture, on a dialectical as opposed to an apodictic conception of philosophy,
now takes form as a distinct shift from poetic to prosaic language in Plato. Such a shift has odd as well as predictable
characteristics.

Thus, according to Gadamer, even when Plato is bad, he is good: "Plato tells his tale 'poorly,' showing no concern for the requirements of any narrative which is intended to absorb the narrator and listener alike in the spell cast by the shapes which it conjures up."[35] The key to understanding why Plato tells his tale poorly and thereby facilitates the possibilities of philosophy lies in the concept of *play*. Six years earlier, Gadamer had introduced the concept of play in his habilitation thesis, but it is only in "Plato and the Poets" that the concept is put to work.[36] Its use can best be understood by recalling, yet one more time, what language, in the thinking of the members of the Stefan George Circle, was supposed to do. Language ideally is not an expression of something outside itself but is rather a framework within which meaning is created. Whenever language is used as a tool to express something outside itself, it lacks play and playfulness. It tends to take on the opposite characteristic of seriousness, and for good reason, we might add. It is no easy business to be a tool, and the practical life of providing food, clothing, and shelter is not a relaxed activity. Hence play has little to do with everyday language.

Put differently, if the poets take their own writing *seriously*, it is because they take it to be the expression of something else. If it is not the expression of something else, then it must be taken *playfully*, for there is no other way to take writing that creates meaning in its own play of words. Once again to Gadamer: ". . . lighthearted play would celebrate that which is taken truly seriously," and this is the ethos of the community.[37] The poetry that Plato objects to, according to Gadamer, is one that claims to be "the soul's representation of self in the mirror of an exalted reality."[38] Hence for Gadamer seriousness enters poetic language and play leaves it when it attempts to imitate an *exalted reality* and when it forgets that it is giving shape to nothing more than the *ethos of the community*. In explaining what he means by this claim, Gadamer says that "only the poet who was really an educator and who really shaped human life could play the game of poetry in real knowledge of what it was about: Only those poets can be taken seriously who do not take their poetry writing to be ultimate."[39]

It might well be conceded that play and playfulness are characteristic of a theory of language that claims that meaning lies within rather than outside of language, but what are we to make of the meaning thus created? Is it not arbitrary, simply the product of language facility and nothing more? Perhaps, but this is not the case with Plato. If we dare use the term *express* after giving it such harsh notices, playful language—indeed, Plato's language—does express and thereby bring into reality something that initially may be within language but is finally a realization of language. This is the human soul, and what happens in playful language is that the soul is first constituted. This idea is at the center of Gadamer's interpretation of Plato's work.

Nowhere is this idea of the constitution of the soul in language better illustrated for Gadamer than in Plato's myths. These for Gadamer are constructed in the teeth of the Greek Enlightenment tendency to reduce myth to natural structures and hence explain them away. In the face of this tendency to "explain the soul itself and to eliminate the mystery which surrounds the powers of justice and love by reducing them to clever (or weak) contrivances or infirmities, Socrates emerges . . . as the visionary who sees his own soul."[40] The important feature of Platonic myths, according to Gadamer, is that they never lose sight of the human soul. They are not entertainment designed to call attention to the soul. "[To] be sure, in these poetic myths the soul does not transform itself into a variety of figures which assert themselves against us while keeping us in ignorance of their truth."[41] The soul rather returns "from its journey through the surreal realms of myth in which Socratic truth rules as the real law of things, chastised and set right in its beliefs."[42] So the journey into myth, literature as it were, is justified by the need to give the soul a *Gestalt*, or form. Yet the Socratic myth is not literature per se but is rather philosophizing: "These [mythical] worlds make all too obvious the importance of its philosophizing, a task from which no revelation . . . sets it free."[43]

The Platonic myths thus lay the groundwork for philosophizing, but this important activity takes place in the dialogues even more than in the myths. Once again, Gadamer reverts to his favored theme of play: "Precisely because of the seriousness of his purpose, Plato gives his mimesis the levity of a jocular play. Insofar as his dialogues are to portray philosophizing in order to compel us to philosophize, they shroud all of what they say in the ambiguous twilight of irony."[44] In this way, Gadamer continues, Plato is able to escape the trap of writing, which is not able to come to its own aid because writing is so definitive. Plato thereby creates a real philosophical literature that is able to refer to something serious beyond itself. Plato's "dialogues are nothing more than playful illusions which say something only to him who finds meanings beyond what is expressly stated in them and allows these meanings to take effect within him."[45]

These references to meanings beyond the language of the dialogues or myths may be taken as problematic, an indication that Gadamer is not holding to the Georgian idea of a pure language, but I do not think the problem is real. Once again, we do well to recall the thread of the irrational in Greek life begun by Nietzsche and continued by Rohde and Freud. I believe Nietzsche's point was that language reflects more than the rational side of life. it also reflects and gives shape to the irrational forces in life, and precisely because these forces are irrational, they have to be shaped in mythological forms which apparently defy any further "rational" explanation. To attempt further explanation is often a matter of "explaining away" and is thus a form of repression. Nietzsche, Rohde, and Freud all argued against this kind of repression, so characteristic of the German nineteenth century, and here we have Gadamer also arguing against it, implicitly, by paying attention to Plato's myths.

And finally, as a way of clinching this particular argument

about Plato's language, Gadamer notes that Plato allows one traditional form of poetry to continue to exist. These are songs of praise for the gods. The reason is that "the song of praise in the form of poetic play is shared language, the language of our common concern."[46] In songs of praise of the gods, there is furthermore "no danger of . . . self-estrangement. . . . In praising, neither the one who praises nor the one before whom the praise is made is forgotten."[47] It is in the nature of praising that the "standard by which we evaluate and comprehend our existence is made manifest."[48]

Thus, in sum, what Platonic myths, dialogues, and songs of praise do is to recall us to the self. these are the forms of language which, like indirect speech, are justified because they are not distractions from the central concern of ethical life, which is the state of the human soul. Language is ultimately revealed to be educational insofar as it has this maieutic power to bring out the soul. It is thus the ideal preface to the idea of Plato's educational state.

IV

The concept of education contained in "Plato's Educational State" has need of being located and contextualized.[49] Hence Gadamer begins this essay by once again returning to the touchstone of Plato's autobiographical comments in the *Seventh Letter*. This time, however, Gadamer treats the *Seventh Letter* explicitly rather than implicitly and focuses its importance in his own autobiography. He notes that the *Seventh Letter* became significant in Plato research in Germany after World War I, and he gives as the reason that it provided a basis for reaching an understanding of Plato's works and his philosophy. He then notes that as a consequence of the enhanced status of the *Seventh Letter*, Plato's *Republic* "came to occupy a more central position than it had ever held before."[50] In sum,

Gadamer is here trying to contextualize Plato's diverse philosophical elements as being political. There is nothing new
here, nothing that was not already done in Gadamer's habilitation thesis and in "Plato and the Poets." Yet it should be emphasized that this continuity, this repetition, is itself significant. It is a hallmark of Gadamer's early writings that Plato is
treated not just as a philosopher who roamed from one department to the next in his philosophical inquiries but that all of
his wanderings make sense only from the same *political* intention. Thus the earlier concerns with ethics and with literature
are related to the concern for education by being tied into the
same political context.

Education is then further located by being tied into the *Republic*, and the main point here is that Plato in the *Republic* is
not intent upon a course of political reform. This too is a familiar topic in the writings of the early Gadamer, so it need not be
elaborated at length. The point is that Plato is not intent upon
reform for the simple reason that the Athenian state is beyond
reform; this much is made clear to Gadamer by the discontinu-
ous discussion of justice in the *Republic's* Book I. This being
the case, Plato shifts his approach and treats the state in a
utopian manner. Gadamer's point here is similar in my opinion to the basic approach taken up in his initial writing on
Jaeger's interpretation of Aristotle's *Protreptikos*. If Plato
were to accept the existing state, his approach to its ethical or
educational problems would be positivistic. He would be looking at established facts and their relationships unquestion-
ingly. He could thus formulate himself in writing and articulate the logic of facts. But Plato intends to question political
facts. The *Republic's* initial book thus demonstrates that the
thing called justice does not exist, or at least does not have a
stable existence. It is not a fact in classical Athens, or put differently, one cannot learn anything worth knowing about justice in Athens by following a positivistic approach. A dialectical approach is adopted because a new concept of justice
must be created. The *Republic* is a dialogue without a final answer to its own question. Its real intention is to engage us in
dialogue.

Let me put this point somewhat differently: Gadamer is here claiming what he had been saying since his early acquaintance with the thinking of the poet Stefan George. If things are taken for granted, then language exists merely as a tool to express them. If, however, the existence of things, like justice, is brought into doubt, then language takes on a greater significance. It does not express things but is rather the locus of the creation of things. This is precisely the case in the *Republic,* where the chief political thing—namely, justice—is very much called into question in Book One, thereby confronting the three conversationalists assembled at the outset of Book Two with the choice of collapsing into relativism or adopting a dialectical approach to politics to replace the discredited positivistic approach. They cannot say what justice *is,* and so therefore they construct it in words. Through dialogue, justice takes on an initial literary shape. The Platonic state of the *Republic* is indeed a utopia.

The Platonic Socrates is not a utopian first and a dialectician second. This formulation gets the logic of cause and effect backwards. The Platonic Socrates is a seeker of knowledge for whom positivism fails. This is what happens in the first book of the *Republic.* The Platonic Socrates only thereafter falls back on a dialectical approach. This makes the Platonic Socrates into a utopian, but utopia here does not mean that the Platonic Socrates is describing some ideal realm that has never existed and never will. It rather has the much more limited sense that Socrates is creating the state in words. If this state is utopian, it is not because it is perfect in some idealistic sense but simply because it exists only in speech, and this admittedly is a tenuous existence. Plato's educational state is the continuation of ethics by other means. Nonetheless, at least in its utopian form, the means are the same as they were for the ethics: words.

The real subject matter of the *Republic* is the soul. Like the state, it is not an entity that has a prior existence that a good positivist methodology can ferret out. Gadamer goes to great lengths to make this point. He does this by denying that there is any such thing as a *nature* to the soul, a move which will of course enable him to deny the positivistic method: "The healthy soul . . . is not simply in the hands of some 'nature' which takes care of it, it does not possess a natural good constitution which could be said to govern it."[51] Then, speaking of justice as well as the soul further on in the same paragraph, Gadamer says that "they are not of a certain 'nature' and are not good by dint of a good 'nature.' This holds for the soul as much as it does for the state."[52]

Because the soul does not possess a *nature*, it logically follows that it needs knowledge of itself. That is to say, if it had a nature, then there would be a tendency toward positivism. We would no doubt reflect on the soul, but ultimately we would test our insights against a wider, more universal theory of nature. Ultimately, that is, the soul would be seen as a microcosmic restatement of laws that prevail everywhere in the natural universe. But Gadamer does not take this approach, and hence the soul's knowledge of itself must be handled differently.

The soul "knows always about the danger of being out of tune because it is knowingly keyed to being in unison with itself. It is always aware of being in tune with itself, which is to say that it is always endangered."[53] So the soul may not have a nature, but it does have something of a supernature in the concept of tonal harmony that is indigenous to it. It does have at least a tendency that gives us guidance and thereby makes creative language something more than merely arbitrary. Gadamer then goes on by noting in distinctly Heideggerian terms that the

> . . . Greeks have a beautiful expression for this inner referencing of the well-constituted soul to *Dasein's* knowledge of itself: *sophrosune*, which Aristotle explains as *phronesis*. With *phronesis* conceived as the knowing self, *Dasein* succeeds in winning a durable governance of itself.[54]

So clearly the point is that the absence of a natural constitution in the soul leads to the requirement that it have knowledge of itself. The law of harmony here prevails. The reflecting soul knows that it has the correct knowledge of itself when it feels itself in harmony. The ultimate purpose of reflection on the soul is to bring this harmony into words.

If I understand Gadamer correctly, I think he is saying that Plato's *Republic* is a *Gestalts*-biography of the human soul. The fact that the Platonic Socrates looks to the larger sign-board of the *polis* does not conflict with this, since the *polis* is in any case a continuation of ethics by other means. Thus a forming in words of the state, which is the manifest theme of the *Republic*, is simultaneously a forming in words of the human soul. Plato's educational state is a literary creation with a purpose. It comes into wordy existence to serve as a mirror upon the soul. It has no purpose beyond this, and so if it enables us to see ourselves better, it has served its purpose. This is Plato's educational state.

Put slightly differently, the soul is constituted as a reflection of the state. The Platonic state, insofar as it is itself the unwritten ethos of the community in which we live, turns out to be something like what Karl Marx meant when he spoke of the economy being the *educator*. Education in this sense is nothing so simple and superficial as the lessons we learn in classrooms or from books. Indeed, these lessons are only possible in terms of how well they fit into the unwritten ethos of the community. The teaching of foreign languages, for example, fails in the United States but succeeds in a country like Holland because in each case the ethos of the community differs. American society does not value highly the learning of foreign languages, and hence the teaching of foreign languages generally fails. The opposite is the case in Holland because the learning of foreign languages is believed to be a matter of national survival. In each case the real *educator* is the ethos of the community.

The substance of Plato's educational state is *justice*, which we can now reasonably take to be a set of unwritten rules, the ethos of the community, which Plato, with his distinctly *literary* method is now, in the *Republic*, putting into words. The essence of this education is not to give advice based upon ex-

perience. This was early ruled out in the *Republic*. Its essence
is quite different: "Only justice can bring about a solid and
enduring state and only he who is a friend to himself is able
to win the solid friendship of others."[55] Plato's educational
state is really a description in words of justice. It is a literary
achievement. When reflected back upon to the soul, it incul-
cates the rules by which the soul comes to be in tune with
itself.

The emphasis on the unwritten rules of the community
finally returns Gadamer to a theme with which he had begun
his early writings. This is that Greece was not a *writing* culture but was rather a speaking culture. Plato's educational
state is not a real thing that can be grasped by the positivistic
methods of the *Altertumswissenschaften*. It is rather a utopia
that exists only in the potential of an idea, and the idea must
first be brought into speech before it can have any hope of reality. That Greece—more accurately, Athens—is still a speaking culture, and the possibility of a *philosophical conversation*
was frankly its only hope of redemption. Certainly, from the
point of view of Germans hoping to redeem themselves in the
1920s, it was the only good reason for studying Greece. The
implied message was that Germans, too, could free themselves
from the rigid, written forms of their civilization by returning
to conversation.

V

The value of the two essays covered in this chapter is not what
they add to Gadamer's habilitation thesis but rather what
they reveal about the author. Obviously, Gadamer's habilitation thesis was about ethics and language, and without doubt
the habilitation thesis was connected to an incipient concept of
the state. Yet many of these themes were not carried to fru-
ition in Gadamer's habilitation thesis, and had they been they

would have distracted from the single overriding theme of articulating a theory of Plato's dialectical mode of constructing an ethics. In the two essays I have covered in this chapter, however, concreteness has been given to the ancillary themes of education, the state, and ethics, and one by-product of this has been added clarity about Gadamer's intentions.

Gadamer's early thinking was very much keyed to the values that were fought over in the philological movement of the German nineteenth century. From April 22, 1777—the legendary day on which Friedrich August Wolf had inscribed himself as a student of philology rather than as a student of some technical field—the purpose of the philological movement had been to counter the fragmenting tendency of modernization by shaping education to the terms of a vision of the ideal whole person. The first generation of German classical philologists had followed this lead and always managed to produce works that were technically flawed but educationally inspiring. The writings of Hölderlin, Schiller, and Goethe are the model writings for this first generation. But with the rise of *Altertumswissenschaft*, a distinctly positivistic and historicist tendency took over and submerged the central literary tendency of the philological movement.

The high point of this movement toward *Altertumswissenschaft* was reached with the arrival of Wilamowitz to the Berlin Chair for classical Greek philology, and the high point of the reaction to this triumph of *Altertumswissenschaft* was spread out over the works of Nietzsche, Rohde, and the thematics of the Stefan George Circle. They recaptured, not always perfectly, the humanist edge that had been lost by academics like Wilamowitz. With German defeat in World War I, the stage was set for a complete return to the original humanistic values of the German philological movement.

Gadamer's early work represents a neglected chapter in that return. Jaeger's *Third Humanism* commanded center stage, but unfortunately Jaeger was not capable of producing the revolution that was needed. He grasped that there was a problem but continued to address the problem in the manner

of an *Altertumswissenschaftler*. He never broke with Wilamowitz, as Friedländer had, and consequently Jaeger placed himself in an ambivalent position from the outset. Gadamer's
work was not paid attention to because he was young and unknown, and it would have been too much to expect that he
would have taken himself more seriously than he did. His
prime interest was in securing a professorship, and this pre-
vented him from seeing and capitalizing on the real import of
his thinking.

The two essays considered in this chapter emphasize the
continuity of the young Gadamer with the values of the early
classical philologists. Greece is valued not for its own sake but
rather for what it could provide in the way of an image of the
ideal self that could stand at the center of the German educational venture. The state is conceived and valued not for its
own sake, which invariably is a concentration of power, but
rather for the sake of what it might contribute to the shaping
of the human soul. Language is conceived and valued for its
immanent power to provide forms which can be emulated. The
vision is nothing if not romantic, in the looser and better sense
of that term.

Yet the distinctive value of these early writings of Gadamer
is not simply in their extension of the romantic project. Their
distinctive value is in recognizing the crisis of the German
philological movement and addressing it philosophically. Indeed, this kind of emphasis points up the decisive difference
between the young Gadamer and the members of the Stefan
George Circle, and it is what makes his early thinking well
worth considering, even today. Where the members of the
George Circle blindly extend the emphasis on literature, on
what Germans like to call *Dichtung*, Gadamer shifts the meaning of this key term and turns it into something more appropriate to the prosaic realities of the twentieth century. Nowhere is this better illustrated than in the essay "Plato and
the Poets," for here we have Plato *exiling* the poets from the
city, and hence taking a direction diametrically opposed to

that of the Georgians, who would put poets at the center of the city.

The relationship between Gadamer and the Stefan George Circle is reminiscent of the conversation between the Platonic Socrates and Ion: Socrates would puncture poetry because the aesthetic consciousness it fosters works against the sober assessment of the real problems of ethics. So too would Gadamer. Ion would rely fully on the mystical meaning of the Poet, and so too the members of the Stefan George Circle. Although not always keyed to poetry, they would certainly have placed the vision of heroic, poetic thinking at the center of their *Reich*. By the 1930s, Gadamer had clearly outgrown his early attachment to the romanticism of the Stefan George Circle.

These considerations enable us to focus the distinctive contribution of Gadamer's early writings. His thinking is not at all romantic in the narrow sense of that term. It is soberly realistic in confronting the spiritual bankruptcy of his times, and he produces a theory of language that is keyed to addressing the problems of Weimar Germany. No values can be presupposed. This is not to say that there were no values in Weimer Germany—that would be an absurd statement—but rather that there was a proliferation of value systems that made Weimar Germany look like a nightmarish projection of the scene described in the first book of Plato's *Republic*. In such a context, there was nothing better to do than ban the ideologues from the city and start from scratch.

Gadamer's habilitation thesis had already proposed something like this, but in a political vacuum. The two last essays move to close that vacuum by addressing themselves directly to the political context of language, but as a matter of timing, they were already too late. "Plato and the Poets" was first published in 1934, one year after the Nazis had come to power, and "Plato's Educational State" eight full years thereafter. They had no chance to begin the debate that would lead to their realization. There is thus, unfortunately, no development of Gadamer's early thinking into political theory. There is movement in the direction of democratic political thinking, and it was recognized by none other than Karl Goerdeler, the Mayor of Leipzig and a central figure in the July 20, 1944, attempt to assassinate Hitler.[56] But nonetheless Gadamer's developing political thinking remained stillborn. It is therefore left to us to complete it.

7

The Early Thinking
of
Gadamer

I

The great achievement of Wilhelm von Humboldt, the reform
of the Prussian educational system, was from the outset a curiously ambivalent affair. He in fact did change the internal
structure of the Prussian state in a way that would seem to
have favored the advent of classical Greek values. But in a remarkably short span of time, the bureaucratic Prussian state
put forth a set of demands that functioned to convert the creative and poetic appropriation of classical Greece by men like
Schiller, Hölderlin, and the other figures of the romantic generation into the flattened and systematic scientism of *Altertumswissenschaft*. Personified in the figures of Böckh and
later Wilamowitz, the new science of the classical world incorporated all the social values of modern natural science
and hence set the stage for the rebellion that began with
Nietzsche.

The ideal classical philologist of *Altertumswissenschaft* was recognizable as a Lockean laborer, clearing away the "rubbish" from the ruins of classical civilization so that "facts" could make themselves felt and patterns could be revealed. The "master builders" of Locke's imagination, men like Newton, had their counterparts in the giants of classical Greece, men like Plato. Locke's intent was to make Newton's "method" plain and simple, and so he reduced it to empiricism. The intent of Böckh and Wilamowitz was to reveal such men to have been products of their times. They, too, had a "method" for doing this, and it was Wilamowitz's claim that he had nothing other than "method" to teach. Clearly, the intent of *Altertumswissenschaft* was to drain away all genius from classical Greece, to effect an *Entzauberung* that would match the demythologization of nature that had taken place in Locke's century. Only then would a true science of the ancient world take shape. It was against this growing academic "normal science" that Nietzsche rebelled.

The Stefan George Circle made a sustained, abstract, and highly emblematic contribution to this Nietzschean genre of cultural criticism. In effect, the Georgians looked for new values, although there is every reason to believe that they did not know what they were looking for or why. If Nietzsche focused on the irrational in Greece as a way of structuring his rebellion against the maddening emphasis on rationality in Greek life, the Georgians made irrationality the hallmark of their rebellion. They were, in sum, cultural critics in the most pessimistic sense of the term.

What concerned the Georgians and fueled their irrationality was the gradual weakening of the German life-world under the impact of advancing bureaucratization and, by the end of the century, industrialization. At best, the German state was fully incapable of addressing this problem. At its worst, the German state was an accomplice to bureaucratization and industrialization. It was hostage to the industrialists of the Ruhr, the bankers of Düsseldorf, and the traders of Frankfurt. But it was also the successor to the already heavily bureau-

cratized Prussian state. Prussia's conquest of the industrializing Rheinland was thus the creation of the worst of possible
combinations. *Altertumswissenschaft* was an aspect of this
bureaucratized, industrializing Germany of the Wilhelmine
period.

For the Georgians, what was called for was a revolution that
would replace the present state with an entirely new one capable of ushering in a new culture. It was never clear to the
Georgians what this new culture should actually look like,
only that it should be modeled on the personality profile of the
leader. Absurdly, they each chose their own favorite leader in
their quest for a figure who would sanction new values in his
actions. And the acts of the various heroes were always so
close to pure act that the Georgians were incapable of translating these actions into prescribed social and political values.
It was an article of faith of the Georgians that none of them
could or would say in advance what the new empire would
look like. To even describe the coming *Reich* would turn it into
something planned, and they wanted none of this. The leader's
Gestalt would fully determine the shape of things to come.

Because Nietzsche was a classical philologist, the Georgians
always retained an interest in the classical model, however,
and in the thinking of Hildebrandt, Friedemann, and Friedländer, they developed a thread of thought that contained a
distinctly different departure. Against the growing scientistic
rationalization of the German life-world, they proposed not an
irrational rebellion but rather a rebellion in terms of a different norm of rationality. They discovered Socrates and Plato as
embodiments of this rationality and hence moved on to conceive these men as *Gestalt* figures. Their models are strikingly
undeveloped or poorly worked out, but this is beside the point
that they initiated a new line of thought among the Georgians. All three were attracted to Paul Natorp for the simple
reason that he too deviated from the established modes of ap-
propriating Plato. Marburg in the early 1920s became the center of this small movement.

It is appropriate at this point to thematize what was happening among the Georgian classicists, and this can be done in terms borrowed from Thomas Kuhn. The Georgians were asking for a "revolutionary science" of the ancient world, one that would effect a paradigm shift away from the model that governed the thinking of the established "normal science" called *Altertumswissenschaft*. They fully understood that the study of Greece in imperial Germany was worse than useless because it was being used to sanctify the bureaucratization and industrialization that was taking place. The paradigm shift that they wanted was one that put forth a distinctly different picture of Greece, one that would defy the categories of scientistic culture. The flattened would again become three-dimensional. The diachronic would take synchronic form, the *zerstückelt* would be restored to a whole, and a world that was dead would again become a recognizable life-world.

They—and I refer to Hildebrandt, Friedemann, Friedländer, and even Natorp—could not effect that paradigm shift. Neither for that matter could Gadamer, as the successor to the above-mentioned classicists, but he went further and did more to give shape to their vision than did any of his contemporaries. He adopted the device of the *Gestalt*-biography but did not exaggerate it. He was deeply informed and enriched by the insights of Martin Heidegger but as a trained classical philologist had a more disciplined grasp on Greece. Also unlike Heidegger, Gadamer was able to give a political twist to his work, by which I mean that he was able to see Plato and the "Platonic Socrates" as thinkers intent upon establishing or reestablishing the life-world of the *polis*. As a result of all these differences, there is a continuous emphasis in Gadamer's early work on the development of practical thinking. It sets him apart.

Gadamer's early writings therefore present an exception to the tendency toward what Weber would call a "perfectionist" ethics. This is not to deny that the Platonic Socrates was a cultural superman. He was cast in this role as early as 1914 by Friedemann. He is, however, not the worst of possibilities. We have now seen Gadamer's Platonic Socrates in his full development, and he is a good sight more palatable than other projected Germanic ethical supermen. Marx's proletariat, Nietzsche's *Übermensch*, the routine *Gestalt* figures of the Stefan George Circle biographies, are all characters distinguished by their superhuman and hence extralegal characteristics. They are "perfect" in their fashion and hence adequate personalizations of the notion of a perfectionist ethics. Gadamer's Platonic Socrates is from the outset much less superhuman, much more willing to assert and emphasize his humanity, much more given to an ethics of responsibility that is not sanctioned by a universal law and hence much better keyed to act as a personalized model of a responsible German state.

Obviously I am urging that there is a similarity between Weber's *Verantwortungsethik* and Gadamer's *dialektische Ethik*.[1] Yet there is also a difference. Weber compensates for the constitutional failings of the German state by imposing an ethical burden of responsibility on the individual. Gadamer goes far beyond this. In the personalized theory of the Platonic Socrates, he constructs an ethical paradigm that is a model for the state and not merely compensation for the constitutional shortcomings of the existing German state. It is not, finally, the individual who is expected to act responsibly in a context in which states do not. With Gadamer it is rather that the portrait of the responsible individual is really a personalized theory of the responsible state. This image is Aristotelian in spirit. It is an image of the *polis* as the continuation of ethics. It is worth looking at in more detail.

II

Take, for example, the profession of ignorance of Gadamer's Platonic Socrates. It represents a brilliant first step insofar as it indicates a superman who is intent upon emphasizing his humanity. It locates a superman who is super for the reason that he does not claim to be intellectually superior. Over against this distinctly human Socrates, all others claim to know what justice is, yet all that they indicate by their professions of superior knowledge is their political narrowness, and hence their actions reveal just how superhuman the Socratic profession of ignorance really is. From the outset, the Platonic Socrates reveals his awareness of the basic pluralism of society and thus appeals to anyone who is not narrow himself in his concept of justice. The Platonic Socrates prefigures a state which is restrained in its claims upon its own citizens and upon other states because it recognizes that it does not have objective truth.

Depersonalization of the literary figure of the Platonic Socrates reveals the theoretical point that the profession of ignorance is but another name for the argument that politics is based on opinion (or prejudice) rather than truth. Therefore politics *as such* is a limited activity, and hence the state (not merely the individual) is duty-bound to act responsibly. This is a theoretical point that is universally applicable, by which I mean that it is not only appropriate to a theocratic state claiming access to divine truths from another world but also to a secular state claiming access to the scientific knowledge of this world. The monolithy of both kinds of states is challenged by the pluralism of the Platonic Socrates. My point, in brief, is that the Socratic profession of ignorance does not escape all forms of absolutism only to fall into relativism. Ironically, it has its own quasi-transcendental quality: It is a finite absolute. The implicit claim of Socrates' vision of politics is that no one possesses the transcendental truth that can serve to put an end to politics as a dialogue.

To push this argument about the Socratic profession of ignorance to its extreme, we have to look at the way it functions in a larger context. It allows the Platonic Socrates to teach political responsibility for the reason that he can hold others *answerable* for their own knowledge claims. Seemingly, the profession of ignorance allows the Platonic Socrates to escape responsibility by hiding behind a feigned ignorance, but Gadamer's Platonic Socrates never really does this. Rather, from the first page of the *Republic* to the last, he allows himself to be repeatedly "arrested" and held *answerable* for his claims. In both respects, then, in holding others answerable and in allowing himself to be held answerable, the figure of the Platonic Socrates is a model for the well-constituted state.

The further development of Gadamer's Platonic Socrates does not belie this brilliant beginning. The very notion of *dialectics* is one that incorporates into one's thinking a theoretical principle of constitutionality, and hence it is the second step, after the profession of ignorance, in articulating a personalized model of a responsible state. To once again depersonalize the dialectics of the literary figure of the Platonic Socrates: Every claim is legitimate only insofar as it opens itself to the real possibility of counterclaim. In Gadamer's German: *Anspruch* gains its legitimacy only insofar as it can tolerate *Widerspruch*. Thus the Socratic profession of ignorance is nicely followed up by a rational procedure, dialectics, which further articulates the principle behind the practice of professing ignorance. That is to say, only because one remembers that one does not really know what justice is can one be open to listen to the counterclaim of the Other in conversation.

In emphasizing dialectics, Gadamer contributes to returning European philosophy to its first form. That is to say, *dialectics* is the appropriate basic form of philosophy because it excludes the prejudice, common to everyday life, that there is (or must be) a truth, conventional or transcendent, which can guide the carrying out of the everyday activity of philosophy. The truth-for-us of philosophy is that there is no truth-as-such which, once arrived at, simply has to be systematized for philosophy to put an end to its own peculiar business. Because there are no exceptions to this, dialectics turns out to be the universal form of Greek philosophy and, I would argue, philosophy itself. Of course, dialectics could itself be brought into question, and such a question would be legitimate, but the question whether dialectics was the universal form of philosophy could only be aired dialectically, and hence even the conclusion that there was a single, universal law that was non-contingent and hence transcendent would itself be contingent upon the dialogue that led up to such a recognition.

Put differently, philosophy ends, if it ends at all, in politics, and this is the case quite simply because *politics* is nothing but another word for the situated, finite, human condition. So therefore philosophy ends where it began, in the human condition, which is just another way of saying that the debate about the *end of philosophy* is itself an illusion. The claim that Plato is an antipolitical philosopher is hence a claim that Plato is not a philosopher after all. But this is not Gadamer's claim. His emphasis on the authenticity of the contested *Seventh Letter* represents the taking of a necessary position in Plato scholarship, and I need not repeat here the argument as to why it is necessary. What needs to be emphasized in the context of this concluding argument is that the Gadamerian vision of politics as reducible to dialectics but then irreducibly tragic (because it cannot be further reduced to an absolute) is yet another instance of the tendency of the thinking of the early Gadamer to accept politics for the imperfect thing it is. Put differently, the refusal to accept politics as irreducibly tragic is the condition of the possibility of perfectionist absolutism. It is the refusal to accept the inescapably tragic human condition that opens the way for absolutism, and the charm of absolutism is its perfectionism: It clearly offers escape from the pain of everyday politics.

Moreover, in the articulation of the constitutional model, the Platonic Socrates of Gadamer is unlike every other German superman of the nineteenth century in that he does *not* want to be alone. He does not want to establish a dictatorship of a single class, the proletariat, or retreat with his animals to a mountaintop in the fashion of Zarathustra, or decisively shape other human beings in terms of a single image, as does the typical *Gestalt* figure of the George Circle. In other words, he has no *Führerprinzip* of ethical leadership. Gadamer's Platonic Socrates wants a conversation partner. He wants someone who will and can effectively oppose him. He is thus, *mutatis mutandis,* asking for a constitutional principle of limitation in the shape of a legitimate opposition party.

The distinction here is subtle and has already been indicated in reference to the idealized Marxian conception of the proletariat: Given the problem of an absence of constitutional restraints on the power of the state, the intellectual development of a superman who rises up to challenge the state is not an improvement in the basic situation if there are no constitutional restraints on the superman. Indeed, the reality of the perfectionist *proletariat* in power or the perfectionist *Führer* in power represents nothing so much as a worsening of the situation because there is no opposition (or opposing principle) to their domination. Once again, the appeal of Gadamer's Platonic Socrates is that he incorporates constitutional restraints from the very outset. He is thus an alternative to the constitutionally unrestrained power state. This is his strongest appeal.

Let me put this third point into different words by emphasizing a distinctly modern characteristic which Gadamer's Platonic Socrates does not possess: *will* power. The profession of ignorance, dialectics, conversation, the emphasis on the irreducible tragedy of politics—all of these features of Gadamer's Platonic Socrates suggest that he cannot possess the Nietzschean will-to-power and is hence not a modern man. What Nietzsche recognized as the quintessentially distinctive trait of the modern man was the capacity to disengage from the everyday flow of life in order to gain control of it. This form of willpower can best be seen in the seemingly naive example of the modern professional: In its twentieth-century definition, a professional is a person who learns to perform one activity, let us say medicine, in terms of objective standards. The physician makes a distinct profession of knowledge. He professes to be acting in a way which is, finally, under the control of will, either the personal will of the physician or the collective will of a medical association or a hospital. This example is naive because it is seemingly beyond reproof: No one would want to put himself under the scalpel of a physician who was anything other than professional in the above sense of the term.

But politics cannot be professionalized in this way without sacrificing something essential to politics. The surgeon in the operating theater is an absolutist, and we would have it no other way, but when the politician begins to act the absolutist, we have—or should have—problems with this behavior. Similarly, philosophy is not a profession that submits to willpower without losing something essential. The philosopher, like the politician, has to be willing to listen to the contradicting argument of an opponent and has to be willing to concede that the opponent may have the better case. Therefore the philosopher, like the politician, must not only profess ignorance in order to avoid the lethal dangers of a profession of knowledge, he must also profess a desire not to be alone, which is but another way of saying that the philosopher, like the politician, must profess to be a cultural being rather than an egoist.

These characteristics of the personality of the Platonic Socrates can easily be depersonalized because, if my informed guess is correct, the Platonic Socrates is himself *already* a personalization of an underlying political theme. He is, as I have stated several times, a literary figure. The Platonic Socrates is anything but the historical Socrates. He is a literary figure and as such the product of Plato's creative mind. But moreover and even more significantly, the Platonic Socrates is so laden with playful Platonic irony that it is impossible for the modern reader to fix this particular *Gestalt* without making some choices. As soon as one makes these choices, as the young Gadamer most certainly did in his habilitation thesis, the *Gestalt* one is talking about becomes one's own. I believe that this is what happened in the 1920s when the young Gadamer chose to write on Plato and the figure of the Platonic Socrates.

Gadamer's Platonic Socrates is in my opinion the embodiment, the personalization, of the theme of *discourse rationality,* and if this theme does not exactly correspond to the stated need to develop constitutional restraints for the power of the modern state, it is close enough to be worth articulating. Discourse rationality does not simply define a set of limits on state power but rather makes—when applied to an individual like the Platonic Socrates—a set of demands on the development of individual character which, if carried out, will result in a figure, a *Gestalt,* who is effectively assertive over against the power of the state. Put differently, it is not enough to guarantee freedom of speech from infringement by the state, as the First Amendment of the United States Constitution does. It is also necessary that the individual be sufficiently developed to make effective use of freedom of speech. This is not simply a matter of skills but is also a matter of will, although the will referred to here is not the same as Nietzsche's will-to-power. Without the intent to be political and the skills to carry out the intent, political rights remain mere hollow legalisms. When this kind of thinking is collectivized, it leads invariably, I would argue, to a theory of legitimate political opposition.

But this is not all: *Discourse rationality* is a term which refers to a culture. It designates a group of individuals—such as Socrates, Glaucon, and Adeimantus—who have already submitted to established discourse norms. When a newcomer— let us say the Thrasymachus of the second book of the *Republic*—arrives on the scene, he does not at first accept the norms of discourse rationality. But gradually, because of the validity of the norms of discourse rationality, even Thrasymachus is compelled to submit. Thus the individual (in our case Gadamer's Platonic Socrates) may provide the model for the culture, but even at the first moment the culture provides the norm for individuals. The relationship between self and culture is also dialectical.

The personalization of discourse rationality in the *Gestalt* of the Platonic Socrates put a brake on Gadamer's political theorizing, however. Indeed, personalization provides a superb example of what it means to displace political theorizing. As a device, there is nothing wrong with the *Gestalt*-biography. But if the displaced political theory ends there, then it can be worse than useless because it can lead to the conclusion that the author is advocating a *Führerprinzip*. In Gadamer's case this is not a problem, for the irreducible incompleteness of the Platonic Socrates compels the reader to look beyond him to the dialogue. This is just another way of saying that the need of Gadamer's Platonic Socrates for a conversation partner is a pointer to the collective nature of discourse rationality.

This is not the place to expand on a theory of the legitimate political opposition. It is mainly a latent possibility of Gadamer's displaced political thinking, no more significant than the latent possibility of the *Fürerprinzip* that is in Nietzsche's vision of the superman. Just as Nietzsche cannot really be saddled with responsibility for Nazism, so too, the early Gadamer cannot be given the credit for the success of the open political system adopted in West Germany after World War II.

III

No less significant than these indications of nascent constitutionalism in the figure of the Platonic Socrates is the relation this literary figure has to value formation in an industrializing society. In a form that was conventional for German thinkers of the time, Gadamer had turned to a superman to apotheosize the values he chose to emphasize. Yet in a markedly unconventional manner, Gadamer's values were not in blind reaction to the modernization process. Indeed, they were surprisingly keyed to the still-inconclusive character of modernization in an industrializing society.

Gadamer connects to the values of modernization at the two points in his early writings where he introduces the concept of *techne*. The more valuable discussion occurs in the unpublished 1930 piece called *"Practisches Wissen."* I do not want to repeat here what has already been said but rather want to note that this particular discussion conveys the constructive way in which Gadamer understands the modernization problematic. He is not blindly opposed to modernization, an opposition which usually takes shape as a hostility to technology and to its attendant instrumental consciousness. Gadamer can accept the need for *techne* because he has a well-developed concept of *phronesis*. Put differently, because Gadamer has a well-articulated concept of *phronesis,* he can effectively set a boundary to *techne* and provide the humanities with a needed rationale, something which no other thinker in Weimar Germany was able to do.

It is at this point that the contrast between the young Gadamer and his mentor Heidegger can most profitably be emphasized. Heidegger, as is well known, joined the Nazi Party and made himself notorious in his *Recktoratsrede* of 1933. He may have distanced himself from the Party in later years, but evidence recently provided seems to indicate the contrary.[2] Gadamer for his part made opportunistic compromises with Nazism, all of them understandable in terms of establishing a career.[3] Unlike Heidegger, however, Gadamer was never an enthusiastic supporter of the Nazi Party or even a mild supporter. Once he had attained his professorship, he offered nothing to the Party. He remained politically neutral and had this neutrality certified after the war when the Soviet occupation authorities accepted him as the first postwar rector of the Leipzig University. Gadamer's record is not heroic or even pretty, but it is certainly not Heidegger's.

I believe the reason for this difference is to be found in the thinking of the two men. Gadamer's thinking differed in key respects from that of Heidegger and provided the basis for substantially different cultural relation to Nazism. The key differences can be approached from the shared concern with a rising technological society. Heidegger saw *techne* as a dominant force in the modern world, one that was expanding away from its narrow base in the fabrication of things into the broader field of shaping the human soul. This universalization of the claims of *techne* was the product of the Western ontological tradition—so Heidegger—and it was a condition so far advanced that little other than *Destruktion* could be advocated.

Heidegger perceived himself as living in a mass society made of mass men who related socially in terms of technical norms. In such a despairing human condition, Heidegger was already inclined to Nazism even before it appeared on the scene as a major social force. Whatever Heidegger's personal or career reasons for joining the Nazi Party, his thinking placed no barriers in his path. In fact, given the success he had already had in his career, one is compelled to believe that it was Heidegger's thinking more than anything else that led him to Nazism.

This is not at all the case with Gadamer, and the contrast stands out most clearly at those few points where a discussion of *techne* brings his thinking into touch with the related thinking of Heidegger. Gadamer is no less opposed to the domination of *techne* in human affairs than is Heidegger, but because he has a stronger concept of *phronesis,* he is able to scribe a sharp line around *techne*. This is not to say that Heidegger had not had the same thoughts on *phronesis*. Everything about his 1923 seminar on Aristotle's *Nicomachean Ethics* suggests that he had already worked out much of what Gadamer said in his 1930 paper. What really distinguished Heidegger's thought from that of his young student was to be found in their conception of philosophy's history.

Both Heidegger and Gadamer drew a sharp distinction between literature and philosophy. Each admired literature because it was true to life, that is to say, three-dimensional in its portrayal of the complexities of human character. Each conceived of philosophy as a move away from literature, a move that was characterized as a "flattening" of the three-dimensionality of literature. The key term each used to describe such a leveling activity was *Begriff,* or 'concept.' That is, philosophy distinguished itself from literature by according commanding position to the concept of things. The concept of something became more important than the thing itself, and if the experience of the thing did not fit the concept, then so much the worse for the experience. In other words, philosophy, with its decisive reliance on the concept, threatened life, or

rather the soul's relation to the life-world. The basic Heideggerian insight is still exhilarating: He perceived everything in
the human condition as a kind of *verkehrte* or upside-down
world in which every mailman and bus driver was a philosopher equipped with a *Weltanschauung* and he, Heidegger, was
the last human being struggling to regain a full-bodied relation to life.

All of these aspects of the *Existenz* thinking of the 1920s
were shared by the teacher and his pupil. But where Gadamer
differed from his master was in his appropriation of Plato, and
for this decisive difference he had the Georgians to thank.
Heidegger drew the line between literature and philosophy
just before Socrates. Therefore his prime literary interest was
in the pre-Socratics and his sharpest criticism was reserved
for the classical triumvirate of Socrates, Plato, Aristotle. In
this respect, Heidegger never broke with Nietzsche. Gadamer,
as we have seen, did break with Nietzsche on precisely this
point, and for this difference he had Hildebrandt, Friedemann,
and Friedländer to thank. Gadamer drew the line between literature and philosophy before Aristotle but after Plato. This
difference in the concept of philosophy's history then made all
the difference in the world in the way Gadamer could construct himself as an *Existenz* philosopher. Plato for Gadamer
is a literary creator. He is not primarily a philosopher interested in concept-formation but is rather an engaged thinker
passionately concerned for politics, or in full-bodied human relationships. His Socrates is never an analytical thinker intent
on cutting up and destroying the true-to-life claims of others.
He is rather the "Platonic Socrates," a three-dimensional
character whose dialectic is aimed at restoring the full-bodied
character of life in the Athenian *polis*.

Recall for just a moment how Gadamer handled the charge
of intellectualism aimed in the Platonic Socrates. In his 1930
paper, he argued that the Platonic Socrates was anything but
an intellectual (read: philosopher) in his handling of moral
questions. He was not trying to separate thought from action.
He was rather insisting that in the good society, thought and

action were harmoniously related and that therefore good actions had to be understood. If anything, the Sophists were the true intellectuals, for it was they who were claiming that thought and action could be so sharply separated that thoughts could be packaged and sold in the marketplace. Socrates was just what he claimed to be in his *Apology*. He was the defender of the ancient values of Athens.

Thematized, this argument looks as follows: The profession of ignorance is aimed at claims to know moral values separated from action. No such intellectual things, or moral "concepts" exist or can exist. The Platonic Socrates then demonstrates the ignorance of nascent philosophers, the all-knowing Sophists. The Platonic Socrates then "thinks" what his fellow Athenians are doing and engages in this activity of thinking without the aid of moral concepts. This necessarily throws the Platonic Socrates into a number of literary games keyed to sketching out this or that facet of Athenian life. The life of the Platonic Socrates is indeed a life of thinking, but the thinking is never for a moment detached from the complexities of Athenian life. He does not submit his thought to intellectual norms of logical consistency but rather submits it to life, and as a result his thinking is itself three-dimensional and true-to-life.

And then Gadamer turns the tables. Anyone who would accuse the Platonic Socrates of intellectualism sheds more light on himself than on the Platonic Socrates. Such a claim originates in the Judeo-Christian prejudice that accords perfection to moral ideas and sees this world as a godforsaken place. From a purely chronological point of view, such a prejudice first came into the world in the form of Aristotelian *Begriffsphilosophie* or concept-philosophy. Can this 1930 argument be used to demonstrate that Gadamer was already rejecting his most famous teacher? I believe so, but that in any case is not my point. My argument is rather that Gadamer's philosophical thinking does not at all lend itself to Nazism. Where Heidegger's startlingly nihilistic thinking places no barrier in his way toward Nazism and may even encourage him, Gadamer's thinking most certainly places a barrier in his way. Everything in Gadamer's thinking points him away from Nazism, not in the direction of mass popular democracy certainly, but surely in the direction of the well-integrated political community. If Gadamer did have a flirt with Nazism, it can only be accounted for in terms of the career ambitions of a young German academic.

These considerations return us, finally, to the reflections on the Platonic Socrates with which we began this conclusion. Almost all of the thinkers who turned to a heroic figure did so in the hope of finding *substantive* values that would work to reverse or overturn the modernization process. They wanted to be told what to do by a leader. Only that obscure line of thinkers running from Natorp to Hildebrandt to Friedemann to Friedländer to Gadamer reversed this tendency by focusing positively on the Platonic Socrates. Each contributed something to the construction of this particular *Gestalt* figure, but only Gadamer provided the kind of systematic unfolding of the character that enabled him to at once escape the perils of romanticism on the one hand and an overly dry academic style on the other.

The key to Gadamer's success is that he emphasized *discourse* values. His Platonic Socrates does not tell us what to do but does tell us how to go about thinking through whatever it is that we are doing. Gadamer has no substantive values to communicate to us through his figure of the Platonic Socrates, but he does have a number of conversational, or discourse, values. In moving in this direction, Gadamer makes his contribution, however modest, to the philosophical debate over modernization.

IV

Ever since Hegel, continental philosophy has distinguished itself from analytical philosophy by rejecting the dominant methods of the natural sciences. Instead of making itself over in terms of the metaphor of handmaiden to the sciences, the continental tradition has looked away from the scientific understanding of a *nature* presupposed to stand over against us to a vision of the humanities for suggestions of a model for philosophy. Arguably, such an effort began for Germans with Herder, who looked to history for guidance in the effort to construct philosophy. The mode then shifted from one humanistic endeavor to another, but what did not change was the insistence that philosophy had to be constructed in terms of a metaphor different from that provided by the analytically oriented natural sciences.

I use the word "continental" as a technical term to refer to a tradition of resistance to the scientistic model of philosophy. In a previous section I compared Gadamer to Max Weber, who I believe would be widely accepted as a conscious political theorist of the tradition of continental philosophy. In this section I would like to take the comparison in a different direction. I would like to compare the thinking of the early Gadamer to that of Mikhail Bakhtin, the Russian literary theorist.[4]

My point here is that Bakhtin demonstrates a latent political thinking very much like Gadamer's. I realize I am going off on a tangent in doing this comparison, but I think the comparison wins significance if it illustrates the strikingly different ways in which politics can be thought in the continental tradition. The concentration on legal and constitutional structures is the characteristic mode of the analytical tradition of political philosophy. It presupposes that by breaking existing political structure down to its parts and showing how and why they work or fail to work, we can come up with answers to guide us in the reconstruction of the political machinery that surrounds us. Basic to whatever analysis is carried out is the presupposition that human nature stands over against the polity in the same way that nature stands over against the science that intends to put it on the rack. Abstract legality, policymaking, ideology, bureaucratic rationalization, and a whole host of other aspects of the analytical political tradition are not the innocent things they first appear to be. They represent forms of *method* consciousness. They each presuppose a human nature that stands over against the state or the policy-maker or the ideologue and which needs, so to speak, to be put on the rack.

The continental tradition in contrast does not take up the mechanical or "work" or *method* metaphor of the analytical tradition. Basically, it is informed by the Hegelian notion of the human spirit (*Geist*), or in its more secularized version, mind (also *Geist*). There is therefore a strong latent tendency in the continental tradition to run to the creative community or the creative individual for a source of values. Bakhtin incorporates much this tendency in his writing, and it leads to results not unlike those of Gadamer.

There is no possible way that the young Gadamer of the 1920s and the 1930s could have known of the writings of Bakhtin, who was living, thinking, and writing in the provinces of the Soviet Union. And needless to say, Bakhtin would not have heard of Gadamer, although there is every reason to believe that Bakhtin was influenced by the same continental tradition as Gadamer was. Indeed, in one of Bakhtin's writings, he actually claims that his thinking finds its origins in the figure of Socrates.[5] Yet in Bakhtin's case, the chosen ethical superman was not Socrates but rather was Jesus Christ. Now Jesus is perhaps the only figure in the history of Western civilization whose life has a claim greater than that of the Platonic Socrates to serve as a model for ethics and for the reconstruction of the modern state along more humanist and less legalistic lines. To my knowledge, the first continental philosopher to develop this direction of thought was the young Hegel, who in his "Spirit of Christianity" introduced the image of Jesus as *Gestalt* figure who stood as a humanist over against the abstract legalism of traditional Judaism.[6]

Like the Platonic Socrates in his relation to the superhuman Platonic doctrine of ideas, Bakhtin's Christ as model figure labors under the burden of the divinity ascribed to him by tradition. The divinity of the Christ figure is both advantage and disadvantage. In a traditional society, it functions to sanctify values that are then passed on by the tradition. But in a modernizing society, the divinity of the Christ figure poses a problem, especially from the point of view of the humanities. In a word, Bakhtin's Christ figure is in need of humanization if he is to succeed as a source of modern values. This was precisely the kind of effort engaged in by David Strauss (that so impressed Nietzsche) and, in different fashion, by Rudolf Bultmann in Gadamer's circle. Now the problem of a divine figure in a desacralized world posed itself for Bakhtin.

Where Gadamer dissociates the Platonic Socrates from the doctrine of quasi-divine objective ideas in order to bring him to life as a *Gestalt* who makes real and not divinely inspired choices, Bakhtin dissociates his Christ from divinity in order to establish his *Gestalt* figure as a real human being making real ethical choices. As long as Jesus is quasi-divine, his choices and actions are not ethical in the strict sense of the term. They have no human pathos in them. They are not real choices. But with his divinity taken away, Jesus, like the Platonic Socrates, emerges as a truly heroic figure—dare one say Promethean—because he is tragic and therefore qualified to make ethical choices. He does not arrive on the scene equipped with already redeemed knowledge claims.

In sum, Bakhtin locates his Jesus as a historically *situated* being, precisely the same thing Gadamer did when he denied to his Platonic Socrates the otherworldly comforts of the Platonic doctrine of ideas. Bakhtin thus facilitates the rethematization of facticity or, put differently, historical situatedness, if for no other reason than that he, like Gadamer, is personalizing his thinking but, unlike Gadamer, is doing it in a Christian literary setting rather than a classical one. Both Bakhtin and Gadamer, but perhaps somewhat more Bakhtin, are narrative thinkers who grasp and communicate theoretical points by means of dramatic personae.

What the dramatic persona of Bakhtin's Jesus demonstrates is that human ethical *values* are not characteristics or possessions of the individual but are rather shared, or communal, qualities. This characterization of values is a fairly significant direction of thought, easy to communicate but difficult to hold in place in the modern West. As long as we in the West conceive values as discrete things, presupposed to exist with or without our agreement, then they become things that we can possess as properties. I speak of *my* values, you speak of *your* values. We become *self*-righteous when offended if for no other reason than that our private property has been trespassed on. I become morally *self*-conscious insofar as my values are distinguished from yours. The frailty, perhaps absurdity, of the Western mind is revealed at those moments when two individuals agree to respect each other's values, treating them in precisely the same manner as a piece of real estate is treated.

Now, the argument that values are shared characteristics is significant because it is so unusual, assuming that it is seriously meant, as I believe it is in Bakhtin. The argument for the shared quality of values is not to be confused with the argument for *social values,* which are similar in look but different in their origin from what Bakhtin is trying to get at. Social values are generally presented as entities that stand over against us, and such a characterization presupposes that society stands over against us in the same way that nature stands over against the scientist in the tradition of method consciousness. Something different is being said by Bakhtin. What I think Bakhtin wants to say is that values do not take on an existential quality until they are agreed upon. Then they become shared values. Prior to this, the individual values we hold are no more the prejudices, or pre-values, idiosyncratic positions waiting to be tested and agreed upon. What Bakhtin's thinking does is shift the focus of our attention in ethical discourse away from monologue and toward the dialectical mode commonly called *conversation.*

As a dramatic persona, the Platonic Socrates does the same thing. He advances his personal values as prejudices and seeks the agreement that would make them shared values. The dramatic persona of Jesus is perhaps even more compelling because tradition burdens him even more heavily than

Socrates with divinity. Bakhtin's secularized Jesus deepens our sense of distinctly human self-consciousness because, through him, we become aware of our individual selves as incomplete beings. Completeness is achieved through values, and values are no more than understandings we share with other human beings. Bakhtin's Jesus is nearly identical with Gadamer's Platonic Socrates but may be slightly more persuasive to us for the reason that the Christian tradition has been somewhat more influential with us than the classical in the construction of the modern world. Thus Bakhtin, like Gadamer, conceives the self and the other as being inseparably linked. The medium that binds the self and the other is also the same: It is language.

Language for Bakhtin is utterance—the German term for which is *Äusserung,* or 'outer-ance.' Language is utterance of our inner selves, of incomplete, idiosyncratic being striving to be complete. Here, as noted, Bakhtin's Jesus is nearly identical with Gadamer's Platonic Socrates. The logical coherence of any individual's *Innerlichkeit* or inner self is complete only within the terms of his or her own discourse. It is revealed to be distinctly incomplete when confronted with the terms of discourse of another individual because it cannot, on its own terms, achieve completeness of understanding. The challenge confronting the individual is then to use language in all its plasticity to reach out and establish a world of shared values with the other. In this vision of language, Bakhtin is not far from saying, with Gadamer, not that ethics are dialectical but rather something much more radical: *that dialectics itself is ethical.*[7]

Hence, Bakhtin can conceive the human universe as a *polyphony* of different and initially uncommunicating voices. A novel by Dostoyevski is, from the perspective of Bakhtin's thinking, much like a dialogue by Plato.[8] Specifically, a novel by Dostoyevski is polyphonous in the way that Book One of Plato's *Republic* is. The author's voice cannot be identified, which is simply a different way of saying that the text is a polyphony of voices. Each voice takes on authenticity precisely because it is not author-determined. As a result, determination of meaning in a novel by Dostoyevski, just as in a dialogue by Plato, is necessarily supplied by the reader. Just as in Gadamer's hermeneutics, the completion of the work of art is not provided in Bakhtin's theory. Hence the creative act that begins with the work of the artist ends with the interpretation of the reader. Bakhtin has been criticized for this emphasis on incompleteness, but the criticism is misconceived. It is precisely here that the genius of Bakhtin's thinking lies.[9]

The charm of the personalized vision of Bakhtin is that it provides a model of a well-constituted state, in his case a Russian state. It appropriates a dramatic persona whose life story is familiar at the grass roots of Russian culture, and reconstructs that story so that it can serve as the personalized foundation for the political modernization of the Russian monolith. It envisages the individual not at all in individualistic terms but rather as a part that achieves completion or fulfillment (and hence real individuality) only in the state that comes about through polyphonous individual efforts. It thus strikes a blow at exaggerated Western individualism while simultaneously striking an even heavier blow at monolithic Russian absolutism.

Gadamer wrote in an Aesopian political language similar to that of Bakhtin, thereby providing the makings of an argument rather than the argument itself. He wrote in this vein until the collapse of the German state in 1945. Then for reasons of his own, he did not return to the drawing board to construct an explicit political theory. His voice, like Bakhtin's voice, represented a claim on a humanistic future more than simply the latest example of the dispirited German (or Russian) tendency to escape the realities of state power by flight into the beauties of perfectionist ethics.

The term "continental," as noted, is a technical term which indicates an approach to thinking best defined by its opposition to the analytical tradition. Put most simply, the continental tradition refers back to the humanities rather than to the natural sciences for guidance. The continental tradition is nonetheless as capable of producing political monsters as is the analytical tradition. It is this because the humanities can easily be construed to be made up of narrative structures describing the lives of supermen, the choice of hero then being left to the individual scholar. The humanities work best when they rise above this circumscribed level to become a dialogue of competing characters, and this presupposes at the least that the humanist is widely and deeply read. The latent political thinking of Bakhtin and Gadamer results in a vision more humanistic than the focus on any individualized superman can be because it incorporates this higher vision of the humanities.

V

Because the early Gadamer was also interested in the development of a personalized model for philosophy—albeit a philosophy that, as the emphasis on the *Seventh Letter* indicates, was integrated with politics from the outset—he articulated a Platonic Socrates who internalized the dialectical principle in the course of his career and hence also provided a model for *philosophical thinking*. Thus politics, which conventionally and at its democratic best is an external dialogue with another, serves also as a constitutional principle for the construction of the internal thinking soul of the philosopher.

In other words, the dramatic persona of the Platonic Socrates does double duty. The outward dialogue of politics becomes the inner dialectic of the well-ordered philosophical soul, and hence from the initial pages of Gadamer's habilitation thesis, where he first mentioned the idea of an educational state, it is unclear whether education, in Gadamer's vision, is supposed to produce a citizen or a philosopher. My point is that the educational function of Gadamer's state is to do both. It is brought into being for the sake of building into the soul the principle of dialogue, the outstanding virtue of which is that it is self-restricting, and this serves both politics and philosophy. The early Socrates of the *Crito* and the *Ion* is an exemplar of the outer principle of dialogue. He is, in his actions, a model for the well-constituted state. The later Socrates of the *Philebos* is a model of the inner principle of dialectic. His thinking is an internalized conversation of the soul with itself. It is a model for philosophy.

Therefore, with the thinking of the early Gadamer we have a strikingly new definition of the famous *Innerlichkeit* of nineteenth-century German intellectuals. Yes, the good man is to retreat from the reality of political power, just as Plato retreated from the reality of power politics in Greece because there was no way to reform that reality. But the Platonic philosopher is not to retreat into a realm of inner beauty which affords escape from political reality. He is, as Plato tells us in the seventh book of the *Republic,* to learn dialectic for the sake of being able to return to the cave of power politics. Neither does the "good German" latent in Gadamer's thinking merely escape from politics. He retreats inwardly in order to construct his soul according to different principles. Those principles differ only in that they speak against the reality of contemporary power politics and describe the constitutional framework of dialectic which, when it reenters the world of action, will serve to restrict the power of the state. Just as the Plato of the *Seventh Letter* retreats from political reality for the sake of conducting a more radical political campaign, so too the Gadamer of the early writings retreats from politics to philosophy for the sake of eventually returning to politics better armed. There is no conflict between politics and philosophy in this formulation.

In "Plato and the Poets," for example, *aesthetic consciousness* is treated as a mode of awareness that was alienated from practical politics. Here Gadamer came as close as he ever would to rejecting the German *Innerlichkeit* that retreated from the exigencies of everyday politics into the beauties of mental contemplation. That this was no accident or exception

in Gadamer's thinking was made clear by the treatment of
language in the same piece. Plato is exiling the poets from the
city because the language they speak furthers the retreat into
the *Innerlichkeit* of aesthetic consciousness. The language
that Plato wants is one that leads away from the beauties of
idealism toward a greater capacity to confront political
reality.

It should be noted that in "Plato and the Poets" the alternative to poetry is not prose but rather a *philosophical conversation*. Thus, reasoning backwards from the concept of philosophical conversation, we also do well to recognize that the
problem with poetry, in spite of the term *aesthetic consciousness*, was never its beauty. The term *aesthetic consciousness*
does not refer to an obsession with beauty but rather with the
lack of a critical faculty. Put slightly differently,the problem
with poetry and with the aesthetic consciousness that characterized its reception in classical Greece was its lack of the dialectical principle, and more specifically, this becomes a philosophical problem because it worked and continues to work
against thinking. By the classical age, Homeric poetry had become a mindless monologue, sung by rhapsodes like Ion who
were possessed, were thus admittedly winged and holy things,
but were not good teachers for the reason that they were not
good dialecticians. An alternative to poetry is thus called for,
and it is *philosophical conversation* for the reason that philosophical conversation incorporates the dialogue principle.

What Gadamer was doing with language in "Plato and the
Poets" was not all that different from what he was doing in his
1927 critique of Werner Jaeger's thinking. There he had made
a distinction between a *writing* culture and a *speaking* culture
and argued that classical Greece was a speaking culture. This
was a roundabout way of claiming that the Aristotelian *Protreptikos* was a dialogue. That is to say, classical Greece had
not resolved its moral problems. It did *not* have the answers to
the problems of the human condition, and hence it was compelled to remain in a condition in which questions had to be
debated. To claim that Greece had *not* resolved its moral prob-

lems, that it had *not* produced definitive answers to questions posed by the human condition—this was but a different way of saying that Greek culture was still aware of its *situated* being. In other words, the Greece being described by Gadamer in the article on Werner Jaeger's thinking was a Greece involved for good reason in a *philosophical conversation.* On the surface, the 1927 piece appears to have nothing to do with the 1934 piece on "Plato and the Poets," but beneath the changing vocabulary there is a remarkable continuity of thought. It is accounted for by the unchanging situatedness of man, which is germane to our question insofar as it concerns the rationale for philosophical conversation.

The identical thought that is expressed differently in the descriptions of Greece as a speaking culture and a culture in need of a philosophical conversation is perfectly keyed to the notion of a responsible state. Therefore, it would seem logical to argue for a responsible state. Instead, in "Plato's Educational State," Gadamer argues on behalf of the constitution of the soul. At first glance, this seems to be a move away from political realism toward the kind of utopian *Innerlichkeit* that characterized so much German thinking in the nineteenth century. Yet it is not, and even in "Plato's Educational State," Gadamer reminds us why. There he speaks of the significance of Plato's *Seventh Letter* for him and his generation, and for one last time in his early writings, reminds us that Plato was not interested in education for its own sake. He was not a mere philosopher of education. His interest in education is rather politically motivated. It is an educational *state* that he is interested in. If Plato were interested in education for its own sake, then his educational state would turn out to be one or another version of the *Kulturstaat,* but it is not.

"Plato's Educational State" is an appropriate final piece for Gadamer's early career for the reason that it demonstrates that politics is indeed the *sine qua non* of Gadamer's interpretation of Plato's philosophy. The political contextualization of philosophy is appropriate because there are few better ways than politics to humanize the soul. Certainly the soul of many a middle-class humanist had already been deeply informed by art, literature, and music but had remained virtually untouched by a sustained and disciplined contact with the situated and hence questioning and questionable world of politics. Without dialectic, that is to say, without the debate that is characteristic of a world that is irreducibly uncertain, all of the other academic disciplines become misleading to the mind.

Is this to suggest that politics rather than music, mathematics, poetry, or the arts is the definitive humanist study? Insofar as politics is more uncertain and hence more humanizing, the answer has to be yes, but I prefer to answer this question more precisely by noting that politics more than any of the other humanist disciplines leads philosophy toward a conception of rationality based on discourse. It thus stands in contrast to conceptions of rationality that are founded, whether on the external certainties of nature, uncontingent mathematical reasoning, or the ethereal beauties of the poetry Plato wanted to banish from his *polis*. The thread of politics that runs through Gadamer's early writings is thus not at all arbitrary and is always fortuitous. Alone among the several thinkers who traced their intellectual pedigree to the poet Stefan George, Gadamer was able to shape a *Gestalt* in the figure of the Platonic Socrates appropriate to the grim realities of politics in the twentieth century, and if this beginning did not lead consistently to the career of political theorist, that is no occasion for regret. The significant fact is that the early Gadamer found a key metaphor for establishing a tough and flexible concept of discourse rationality, and this provided him the resource he needed to move on to the philosophical hermeneutics of *Truth and Method*.

Notes

Chapter 1

1. Hans-Georg Gadamer, *Truth and Method* (New York: Continuum, 1975). The German original is *Wahrheit und Methode* and is published separately (Tübingen: J. C. B. Mohr [Paul Siebeck], 1960) or as volume 1 of the newly published *Gesammelte Werke* (Tübingen: J. C. B. Mohr [Paul Siebeck], 1985).

2. Hans-Georg Gadamer, *Philosophical Hermeneutics* (Berkeley: University of California Press, 1976). The Introduction by David E. Linge is especially good.

3. Hans-Georg Gadamer, *Dialogue and Dialectic* (New Haven: Yale University Press, 1980).

4. Hans-Georg Gadamer, *Hegel's Dialectic* (New Haven: Yale University Press, 1971); *Reason in the Age of Science* (Cambridge, MA: MIT Press, 1981).

5. Hans-Georg Gadamer, *The Idea of the Good in Plato and Aristotle* (New Haven: Yale University Press, 1986); *Philosophical Apprenticeships* (Cambridge, MA: MIT Press, 1985).

6. Surprisingly, Gadamer's *German* reception history does not differ significantly from his American. He became well known as a consequence of the 1960 publication of *Truth and Method,* and thereafter his

194 Political Hermeneutics

early writings were reissued to be read in the light of his major work. For example, *Platos dialektische Ethik* was reissued in 1968, 1983, and 1985. I was told by a Heidelberg professor who was then a student that in 1960 Gadamer was taken to be a "Loser," as a man whose time had come and gone without a major intellectual achievement.

7. Hans-Georg Gadamer, "Das Wesen der Lust in den platonischen Dialogen" (unpublished doctoral thesis, a typescript copy of which is in the library of the Philosophical Seminar in Heidelberg). I shall not treat the doctoral dissertation in detail in this study because it is not an outstanding work. In routine fashion, it takes a single theme—*Lust,* or desire—and traces it as a thread through all of Plato's writings.

8. Hans-Georg Gadamer, *"Der aristotelische PROTREPTIKOS und die entwicklungsgeschichtliche Betrachtung der aristotelischen ETHIK,"* in *Gesammelte Werke,* vol 5.

9. Hans-Georg Gadamer, *Platos dialektische Ethik,* in *Gesammelte Werke,* vol. 5.

10. Hans-Georg Gadamer, "Plato und die Dichter," in *Gesammelte Werke,* vol. 5. The English translation of this piece is "Plato and the Poets" and is in Gadamer, *Dialogue and Dialectic.*

11. Hans-Georg Gadamer, *"Platos Staat der Erziehung,"* in *Gesammelte Werke,* vol. 5. The English version is "Plato's Educational State," in *Dialogue and Dialectic.*

12. Author's conversation with Gadamer, Heidelberg, August 1985.

13. Especially valuable is *"Die neue Platoforschung,"* in Gadamer, *Gesammelte Werke,* vol. 5. This review article indicates how diligently the early Gadamer kept abreast of current thinking on Plato.

14. Gadamer, *Gesammelte Werke,* 5:212–29.

15. Gadamer, *Gesammelte Werke,* 5:230–48.

16. For such an argument, see chapter 7.

17. There are of course exceptions. See, for example, Richard Bernstein's *Beyond Objectivism and Relativism* (Philadelphia: University of Pennsylvania Press, 1983).

18. Werner Jaeger, *Aristotle* (New York: Oxford University Press, 1934, 1962, 1967). First published in Berlin in 1923.

19. Unfortunately this sentence is omitted by Gadamer in the reprint of his habilitation thesis in the *Gesammelte Werke.* But it is to be found in the original edition. See Hans-Georg Gadamer, *Platos dialektische Ethik* (Leipzig: Felix Meiner Verlag, 1931; Hamburg, 1968, 1984), xv.

20. Author's conversation with Gadamer, Heidelberg, August 1985.

Chapter 2

1. Hans-Georg Gadamer, "Das Wesen der Lust nach den platonischen Dialogen" (typescript in the Library of the Philosophical Seminar of the University of Heidelberg).

2. Paul Natorp, *Platos Ideenlehre* (Darmstadt: Wissenschaftliche Buchgesellschaft, 1961).

3. Ferdinand de Saussure, *Course in General Linguistics* (New York: McGraw-Hill, 1959), as well as Jonathan Culler, *Saussure* (Hassocks, Sussex: Harvester Press, 1976).

4. For Gadamer's opinion on Natorp's unusual reception, see his *"Die neue Plato Forschung,"* first published in 1933, in Hans-Georg Gadamer, *Gesammelte Werke* (Tübingen: J. C. B. Mohr, 1985), 5:228n.

5. See Hans-Georg Gadamer, *Philosophical Apprenticeships* (Cambridge, MA: MIT Press, 1985), 11.

6. Paul Natorp, *"Uber Platos Ideenlehre"* (Berlin: Pan-Verlag Rolf Heise, 1925). This is a reprint of the 1913 lecture delivered to the Kant Society of the University of Berlin. The *"Metakritischer Anhang"* is in Natorp, *Platons Ideenlehre.*

7. For an excellent biography of Herder, see Robert T. Clark, *Herder* (Berkeley: University of California Press, 1955).

8. Here I follow the argument of Ernst Cassirer, *The Philosophy of Symbolic Forms* (New Haven: Yale University Press, 1953), chap. 1.

9. The classic study is Eliza M. Butler, *The Tyranny of Greece over Germany* (New York: Macmillan, 1935).

10. See Wilhelm Böhm, *Schillers "Briefe uber die aesthetische Erziehung der Menschen"* (Halle: M. Niehmeyer, 1927), as well as Ernst Cassirer, *Idee und Gestalt* (Berlin: B. Cassirer, 1921).

11. Fritz Stern, *The Failure of Liberalism* (New York: Knopf, 1972), 3–25, as well as Fritz Stern, *The Politics of Cultural Despair* (Berkeley: University of California Press, 1961).

12. For this definition of philology, see August Böckh, *On Interpretation and Criticism* (Norman: University of Oklahoma Press, 1968), 12, where Böckh uses this phrase for the first time. This is a translation of the first chapter of Böckh's *Encyklopädie und Methodologie der philologischen Wissenschaften* (Leipzig: Teubner, 1877), unquestionably the most influential writing on methodology in German nineteenth-century classical philology. Here Böckh argued that the task of *Altertumswissenschaft* was to reconstruct the mind of the ancient world. The reconstruction was to be undertaken in a thoroughly positivistic manner: Through the sheer accumulation of facts, the outlines of the classical mind would emerge.

13. Böckh's great work of this type has been translated as *The Public Economy of Athens* (London: J. Murray, 1828).

14. For Böckh's engagement with politics, see *Festrede auf der Universität zu Berlin*, 1855, the telling subtitle of which is *Über das Verhältnis der Wissenschaft zu Staat und Fürst* [On the Relationship of Science to State and Prince].

15. Gadamer, *Philosophical Apprenticeships*, 14–15.

16. Richard Bernstein, *Beyond Objectivism and Relativism* (Philadelphia: University of Pennsylvania Press, 1985), 265.

17. There is not yet an adequate treatment of Stefan George and his Circle in the English language, but a good beginning has been made in Michael M. Metzger and Erika A. Metzger, *Stefan George* (New York: Twayne, 1972). The most interesting German work on Stefan George in respect to language is Jürgen Wertheimer, *Dialogisches Sprechen im Werke Stefan Georges* (Munich: Wilhelm Fink Verlag, 1978).

18. Stefan George, *Das Reich* (Berlin: Bondi, 1929).

19. See Siegfried Kaehler, *Wilhelm von Humboldt und der Staat* (Berlin: R. Oldenbourg, 1927). Also, Gebhardt Bruno, *Wilhelm von Humboldt als Staatsmann* (Stuttgart: J. G. Cotta, 1896, 1899), 2 vols.

20. Here I follow Ferdinand de Saussure, *Course in General Linguistics* (New York: McGraw-Hill, 1959), 101ff. and 140ff.

21. Heinrich Friedemann, *Plato Seine Gestalt* (Berlin: Blatter für die Kunst, 1914).

22. Hans-Georg Gadamer, "Die Wirkung Stefan Georges auf die Wissenschaft" (typescript, 1983).

23. See Eduard Spranger's Books, especially *Wilhelm von Humboldt und die Humanitätsidee* (Berlin: Reuther, 1909). For the idea of the German university in the nineteenth and early twentieth centuries, see Fritz Ringer's *The Decline of the German Mandarins* (Cambridge, MA: Harvard University Press, 1969). Ringer is a sociologist of knowledge with a definite ax to grind. But the book is still excellent.

24. It was Nietzsche's opinion that the revolution in German classical philology began with Wolf's registration in 1777. See Hugh Lloyd-Jones, "Nietzsche and the Study of the Ancient World," in James C. O'Flaherty et al., *Studies in Nietzsche and the Classical Tradition* (Chapel Hill: University of North Carolina Press, 1976), 4.

25. Friedrich Nietzsche, *The Birth of Tragedy* (New York: Random House, 1967). Nietzsche is somewhat mistakenly given credit for initiating the modern concern with the irrational side of the Greeks in this book. Nietzsche might not have known of Humboldt's concern for this side of the ancient world, but he most certainly would have been well acquainted with the *Symbolik und Mythologies der alten Völker, besonders der Griechen* (1810–12) of G. F. Creuzer. For the definitive English-

language treatment of this theme, see E. R. Dodds, *The Greeks and the Irrational* (Berkeley: University of California Press, 1951).

26. See Karl-Friedrich Gründer, *Der Streit um Nietzsche's Geburt der Tragödie* (Hildesheim: G. Olms, 1969).

27. Erwin Rohde, *Psyche* (New York: Harper & Row, 1966). This book was in its eighth German edition by 1921 and was translated and published in the United States for the first time in 1925.

28. Gründer, *Streit*.

29. Gründer, *Streit*.

30. On the attitudes of Wilamowitz, see Manfred Landfester's "Ulrich von Wilamowitz-Moellendorff und die hermeneutische Tradition des 19. Jahrhunderts," in Hellmut Flashar, Karlfried Gründer, and Axel Horstmann, *Philologie und Hermeneutik im 19. Jahrhundert* (Göttingen: Vandenhoeck & Ruprecht, 1979). But Wilamowitz is not the originator of this method consciousness in classical philology. It is also to be found writ large in the first chapter of Böckh's *Encyklopädie*.

31. See Kurt Hildebrandt, "Wilamowitz und Hellas," in Peter Landmann and Gunhild Günther, *Stefan George und Sein Kreis* (Hamburg: Hauswedell, 1976).

32. Ulrich von Wilamowitz-Moellendorff, *Platon* (Berlin: Weidemann, 1919, 1920), 2 vols.

33. Werner Jaeger, *Humanistische Reden und Vorträge* (Berlin: Walter de Gruyter, 1960). These are, as the German title indicates, speeches and presentations, but in both cases they are enthusiastic portrayals of Greek thinking and its value for education.

34. On Usener, see Flashar, *Philologie und Hermeneutik*, 160–63.

35. Werner Jaeger, *Aristotle* (New York: Oxford University Press, 1967).

36. Werner Jaeger, *Paideia* (New York: Oxford University Press, 1963), 3 vols.

37. For a brief overview of the controversy, see Majorie Grene, *A Portrait of Aristotle* (Chicago: University of Chicago Press, 1963), chap. 1.

38. William Musgrave Calder, III, "The Credo of a New Generation: Paul Friedländer to Ulrich von Wilamowitz-Moellendorff," *Antike und Abendland* 26 (1980).

39. For what Nietzsche meant by the historical, see James Whitman, "Nietzsche and the Magisterial Tradition of German Classical Philology," in *Journal of the History of Ideas* (July-September 1986), 453–68.

40. Gadamer, *"Die Wirkung Stefan Georges auf die Wissenschaft"* (typescript, 1983).

Chapter 3

1. Otto Kaus, *Dostoevski und sein Schicksal* (Berlin: E. Laub, 1923).

2. Hans-Georg Gadamer, *"Der aristotelische PROTREPTIKOS und die entwicklungsgeschichtliche Betrachtung der aristotelischen Ethik,"* in Hans-Georg Gadamer, *Gesammelte Werke* (Tübingen: J. C. B. Mohr, 1985), vol. 5.

3. Werner Jaeger, *Aristotle* (New York: Oxford University Press, 1967).

4. Plato's *Philebos* in Edith Hamilton and Huntington Cairns, *The Collected Dialogues of Plato* (Princeton: Princeton University Press, 1982).

5. Gadamer, *Gesammelte Werke*, 5:172.

6. Gadamer, *Gesammelte Werke*, 5:172.

7. Richard Bernstein, *Beyond Objectivism and Relativism* (Philadelphia: University of Pennsylvania Press, 1983), 265.

8. For example, Stanley Fish, *Is There a Text in This Class?* (Cambridge, MA: Harvard University Press, 1980), perhaps the leading text of the reader-response movement in the United States. I might note at this point that my use of the term *truth* in this paragraph should not suggest that I necessarily take it to be relative to time and place. If there is a *divine truth*, it certainly need not be contingent. But if we are speaking of *human truth*, then that would have to be relative to time (and place), at least in Gadamer's thinking.

9. Otto Apelt, *Beiträge zur Geschichte der griechischen Philosophie* (Leipzig: Teubner, 1891), 1, 17, 18, and especially 31–37.

10. Gadamer, *Gesammelte Werke*, 5:174.

11. Gadamer, *Gesammelte Werke*, 5:176.

12. Gadamer, *Gesammelte Werke*, 5:176.

13. Gadamer, *Gesammelte Werke*, 5:177.

14. Hans-Georg Gadamer, *Das Wesen der Lust* (typescript in the Library of the Philosophical Seminar in Heidelberg).

15. Gadamer, *Gesammelte Werke*, 5:177.

16. Gadamer, *Gesammelte Werke*, 5:178.

17. Gadamer, *Gesammelte Werke*, 5:167.

18. Hans-Georg Gadamer, *Platos dialektische Ethik*, in Gadamer, *Gesammelte Werke*, vol. 5.

19. Gadamer, *Gesammelte Werke*, 5:5.

20. Gadamer, *Gesammelte Werke*, 5:8.

21. Hans-Georg Gadamer, *Platos dialektische Ethik* (Hamburg: Felix Meiner Verlag, 1983). This is a reprint of the 1931 edition.

22. Gadamer, *Gesammelte Werke*, 5:8.

23. Gadamer, *Gesammelte Werke*, 5:8.

24. Gadamer, *Gesammelte Werke*, 5:9.

25. Gadamer, *Gesammelte Werke,* 5:9.
26. Gadamer, *Gesammelte Werke,* 5:10.
27. Gadamer, *Gesammelte Werke,* 5:10.
28. Gadamer, *Gesammelte Werke,* 5:9–10.
29. Gadamer, *Gesammelte Werke,* 5:14.
30. Gadamer, *Gesammelte Werke,* 5:5.
31. Richard Bernstein, *Beyond Objectivism and Relativism* (Philadelphia: University of Pennsylvania Press, 1983), 265.
32. See A. E. Taylor, *Socrates* (New York: Anchor Books, 1953).
33. Gadamer, *Gesammelte Werke,* 5:5–6.
34. Gadamer, *Gesammelte Werke,* 5:6. See also Gadamer's "Dialectic and Sophism in Plato's *Seventh Letter,*" in Hans-Georg Gadamer, *Dialogue and Dialectic* (New Haven: Yale University Press, 1980).
35. Gadamer, *Gesammelte Werke,* 5:7.
36. Gadamer, *Gesammelte Werke,* 5:6.
37. Gadamer, *Gesammelte Werke,* 5:6.
38. Gadamer, *Gesammelte Werke,* 5:13.
39. Gadamer, *Gesammelte Werke,* 5:13.
40. Heinrich Friedemann, *Platon seine Gestalt* (Berlin: Bondi, 1914).
41. Gilles Deleuze, *Nietzsche and Philosophy* (New York: Columbia University Press, 1983), 8–10.

Chapter 4

1. Hans-Georg Gadamer, *Gesammelte Werke* (Tübingen: J. C. B. Mohr [Paul Siebeck], 1985), 5:15–73.
2. Gadamer, *Gesammelte Werke,* 5:15.
3. Gadamer, *Gesammelte Werke,* 5:18, n. 3.
4. Gadamer, *Gesammelte Werke,* 5:16.
5. It certainly helps Gadamer's case that the Greek term *logos* serves to designate *theory* as well as *language* and *word*. Hence the claim that theory precedes facts can be rendered as: In the beginning was the word, and the word was made flesh.
6. Gadamer, *Gesammelte Werke,* 5:23.
7. Gadamer, *Gesammelte Werke,* 5:23.
8. Precisely this kind of determination of practical philosophy—human situatedness in the world—is fundamental to the thinking of another 1920s student of Heidegger, namely, Hannah Arendt. See Arendt's *The Human Condition* (Chicago: University of Chicago Press, 1958).
9. Gadamer, *Gesammelte Werke,* 5:25.
10. For example, at the beginning of section three, where Gadamer writes . . . [s]elbst wo es nicht zum Aussprechen und Verlautbaren kommt, im DENKEN, denkt man in einer Sprache, die als Sprache auf mögliche

Andere verweist, die dieselbe Sprache sprechen und daher meine GE-DANKEN verstehen würden, wenn sie IN IHNEN LESEN könnten. Gadamer, *Gesammelte Werke,* 5:27.

11. Gadamer, *Gesammelte Werke,* 5:27–33.

12. Gadamer, *Gesammelte Werke,* 5:27. Probably the best translation of the title of Gadamer's third section (*Die mitweltlichen Motive der Sachlichkeit*) would be "The Communal Motivs of Thingness [Objectivity]."

13. Gadamer, *Gesammelte Werke,* 5:33.

14. Gadamer, *Gesammelte Werke,* 5:32–33.

15. Gadamer, *Gesammelte Werke,* 5:32, n. 7.

16. Gadamer reviewed Löwith's habilitation thesis when it was first published. See Hans-Georg Gadamer, *Gesammelte Werke* (Tübingen: J. C. B. Mohr [Paul Siebeck], 1987), 4:234–39.

17. Gadamer, *Gesammelte Werke,* 5:33.

18. Gadamer, *Gesammelte Werke,* 5:38.

19. Gadamer, *Gesammelte Werke,* 5:40.

20. Gadamer, *Gesammelte Werke,* 5:41–42.

21. Gadamer, *Gesammelte Werke,* 5:44ff.

22. Gadamer, *Gesammelte Werke,* 5:45.

23. Fritz Ringer, *The Decline of the German Mandarins* (Cambridge, MA: Harvard University Press, 1967).

24. Thomas Kuhn, *The Structure of Scientific Revolutions* (Chicago: University of Chicago Press, 1961).

Chapter 5

1. In Hans H. Gerth and C. Wright Mills, *From Max Weber* (New York: Oxford University Press, 1966). An excellent discussion of the classical relation of ethics to politics is to be found in Jürgen Habermas's "The Classical Doctrine of Politics in Relation to Social Philosophy," in Habermas's *Theory and Politics* (Boston: Beacon Press, 1974). For a recent discussion of the classical doctrine of ethics, see Martha Nussbaum's *The Fragility of Goodness: Luck and Ethics in Greek Tragedy and Philosophy* (New York: Cambridge University Press, 1986).

2. The German term *Gesinnungs* means "conviction" or "principled" but has come to be translated as "perfectionist" when combined with the term ethics. Quote is from Hans-Georg Gadamer, *Platos dialektische Ethik* (Hamburg: Felix Meiner Verlag, 1983), xv.

3. Gadamer says as much in "Plato and the Poets," *Dialogue and Dialectic* (New Haven: Yale University Press, 1980), 52, 70.

4. Gadamer, *Gesammelte Werke,* 5:230–48.

5. Gadamer, *Gesammelte Werke,* 5:230.

6. In Fred R. Dallmayr and Thomas A. McCarthy, *Understanding*

and *Social Inquiry* (Notre Dame, IN: Notre Dame University Press, 1977), 159–88.

7. Gadamer, *Gesammelte Werke*, 5:248.
8. Gadamer, *Gesammelte Werke*, 5:248.
9. Bruno Snell, *The Discovery of Mind* (New York: Dover, 1982).
10. Gadamer, *Gesammelte Werke*, 5:239–40.
11. Gadamer, *Gesammelte Werke*, 5:239.
12. Gadamer, *Gesammelte Werke*, 5:242.
13. Gadamer, *Gesammelte Werke*, 5:231.
14. Gadamer, *Gesammelte Werke*, 5:232.
15. J. A. K. Thomson, *The Ethics of Aristotle* (New York: Penguin Books, 1978).
16. Gadamer, *Gesammelte Werke*, 5:241.
17. Gadamer, *Gesammelte Werke*, 5:241–42.
18. Gadamer, *Gesammelte Werke*, 5:242.
19. Gadamer, *Gesammelte Werke*, 5:234.
20. Gadamer, *Gesammelte Werke*, 5:243.
21. Gadamer, *Gesammelte Werke*, 5:244.
22. Gadamer, *Gesammelte Werke*, 5:248.

Chapter 6

1. Hans-Georg Gadamer, "Plato and the Poets," in *Dialogue and Dialectic*, trans. Christopher Smith (New Haven: Yale University Press, 1980). The original German version can be found in Hans-Georg Gadamer, *Gesammelte Werke* (Tübingen: J. C. B. Mohr [Paul Siebeck], 1985), 5:187–211. My citations will be from the translated version.
2. Gadamer, "Plato and Poets," 65. See Christopher Smith's footnote for elaboration.
3. Hans-Georg Gadamer, "Plato's Educational State," in *Dialogue and Dialectic*, trans. Christopher Smith (New Haven: Yale University Press, 1980), 73–92. The German version can be found in Gadamer, *Gesammelte Werke*, 5:249–62. My citations will be from the translated version.
4. Gadamer, "Plato and Poets," 48.
5. Gadamer, "Plato and Poets," 49.
6. Gadamer, "Plato and Poets," 50.
7. Gadamer, "Plato and Poets," 50.
8. Gadamer, "Plato and Poets," 50.
9. Gadamer, "Plato and Poets," 48.
10. Gadamer, "Plato and Poets," 48.
11. Gadamer, "Plato and Poets," 51–52.
12. Gadamer, "Plato and Poets," 48.

13. Gadamer, "Plato and Poets," 49.

14. Gadamer, "Plato and Poets," 66.

15. Gadamer, "Plato and Poets," 67.

16. Gadamer, "Plato and Poets," 63–64.

17. Gadamer, "Plato and Poets," 64. All the references to the *self* occur here.

18. Gadamer, "Plato and Poets," 65.

19. Gadamer, "Plato and Poets," 47.

20. Gadamer, "Plato and Poets," 65.

21. Gadamer, "Plato and Poets," 63.

22. Gadamer, "Plato and Poets," 47.

23. Gadamer, "Plato and Poets," 47.

24. Gadamer, "Plato and Poets," 63.

25. Gadamer, "Plato and Poets," 42.

26. Gadamer, "Plato and Poets," 42.

27. Gadamer, "Plato and Poets," 44.

28. Gadamer, "Plato and Poets," 44.

29. Gadamer, "Plato and Poets," 44.

30. Gadamer, "Plato and Poets," 44–45.

31. Gadamer, "Plato and Poets," 45.

32. Plato's *Republic*, 336 b. The citations will fit any edition.

33. Plato's *Republic*, 350 d.

34. Plato's *Republic*, 354 a.

35. Gadamer, "Plato and Poets," 68–69.

36. Gadamer, "Plato and Poets," 50, 58, 66, 68, 69, 70, 71.

37. Gadamer, "Plato and Poets," 66.

38. Gadamer, "Plato and Poets," 68.

39. Gadamer, "Plato and Poets," 60.

40. Gadamer, "Plato and Poets," 69.

41. Gadamer, "Plato and Poets," 70.

42. Gadamer, "Plato and Poets," 70.

43. Gadamer, "Plato and Poets," 70.

44. Gadamer, "Plato and Poets," 70.

45. Gadamer, "Plato and Poets," 71.

46. Gadamer, "Plato and Poets," 66.

47. Gadamer, "Plato and Poets," 65.

48. Gadamer, "Plato and Poets," 66.

49. Gadamer, "Plato's Educational State."

50. Gadamer, "Plato's Educational State," 73.

51. Gadamer, "Plato's Educational State," 88.

52. Gadamer, "Plato's Educational State," 89.

53. Gadamer, "Plato's Educational State," 88–89.

54. Gadamer, "Plato's Educational State," 76, where Gadamer discusses the utopian aspects of the Platonic state.

55. Hans-Georg Gadamer, *Philosophical Apprenticeships* (Cambridge, MA: MIT Press, 1985), 98.

56. Gadamer, *Philosophical Apprenticeships,* 98–99.

Chapter 7

1. H. H. Gerth and C. Wright Mills, *From Max Weber* (New York: Oxford University Press, 1946), 77–129.

2. See Victor Farias, *Heidegger et le Nazism* (Paris: Editions Verdier, 1987).

3. See Sheldon Wolin, "Philosophical Apprenticeships," *New York Times Sunday Book Review,* 28 July, 1985, sect. VII, 12:1.

4. For my thoughts on Bakhtin, I am endebted to Joseph Frank's piece called "The Voices of Mikhail Bakhtin" in the *New York Review of Books,* 23 October, 1986, and to Katerina Clark and Michael Holquist's *Mikhail Bakhtin* (Cambridge, MA: Harvard University Press, 1984).

5. Bakhtin's key concept of the *polyphonic* novel is especially interesting because of his attempt to trace it back to Socrates or, more specifically, to the Platonic attempt to balance conversation by giving the opponents of Socrates the best possible statement of their positions. See Mikhail Bakhtin, *Problems of Dostoevsky's Poetics* (Minneapolis: University of Minnesota Press, 1984), chap. 4.

6. G. W. F. Hegel, *Early Theological Writings,* trans. T. M. Knox (Philadelphia: University of Pennsylvania Press, 1981).

7. See Tzvetan Todorov, *Mikhail Bakhtin: The Dialogical Principle* (Minneapolis: University of Minnesota Press, 1984).

8. Bakhtin, *Problems,* chap. 8.

9. Frank's otherwise excellent analysis of Bakhtin breaks down at the point where the greatest rewards are to be harvested. Instead of following Bakhtin to the implied conclusion that the work of art is by its nature (as a work of art) incomplete, Frank imposes his own prejudice in favor of completeness and then labels Bakhtin a failure. See Frank, "Voices," 59.

Index